Aged in Oak

THE STORY OF THE
SANTA BARBARA COUNTY WINE INDUSTRY

Aged in Oak

THE STORY OF THE
SANTA BARBARA COUNTY WINE INDUSTRY

Otis L. Graham, Jr.
Sarah Harper Case
Victor W. Geraci
Susan Goldstein
Richard P. Ryba
Beverly J. Schwartzberg

Published by
Santa Barbara County Vintners' Association

Featuring the photography of
Kirk Irwin

South Coast Historical Series
Graduate Program in Public Historical Studies
University of California, Santa Barbara
1998

Written by:
Graduate Program in Public Historical Studies
University of California, Santa Barbara
Santa Barbara, California 93106

Published by:
Santa Barbara County Vintners' Association
P.O. Box 1558
Santa Ynez, California 93460

Produced by:
Cachuma Press
P.O. Box 560
Los Olivos, California 93441

Project Coordinator: Pam Maines Ostendorf
Editor: Sue Irwin
Graphic Design: Katey O'Neill
Maps: Sue Irwin
Printing: Tien Wah Press, Singapore

First Edition, April 1998

Library of Congress Catalog Card Number: 97-062455

ISBN: 0-9661897-0-1

South Coast Historical Series
Public Historical Studies Program
University of California, Santa Barbara
List of publications:
Aged in Oak: The Story of the Santa Barbara County Wine Industry (1998)
Stearns Wharf: Surviving Change on the California Coast (1994)
Sifting through the Ashes: Lessons Learned from the Painted Cave Fire (1993)
Casa de la Guerra: A Study in Time and Place (1990)
Public Justice: A History of the Santa Barbara County District Attorney's Office, 1850-1985 (1988)
Santa Barbara's El Presidio (1986)
The Homefront: Santa Barbara During World War II, 1941-1945 (1982)
Studies in a Growing Community: Santa Barbara, 1930-1980 (1982)
Santa Barbara by the Sea (1982)
A History of Environmental Review in Santa Barbara County (1981)
Environmental Hazards and Community Response: The Santa Barbara Experience (1979)
Old Town, Santa Barbara: A Narrative History of State Street from Gutierrez to Ortega, 1850-1975 (1977)

❧ FRONT COVER: LIVE OAK BRANCHES FRAME A SUNNY VIEW OF VINEYARDS IN THE SANTA MARIA VALLEY.
BACK COVER: MANY WINE VARIETALS ARE AGED IN OAK BARRELS.P
HALF-TITLE, PAGE i: A LONE OAK GRACES VINEYARD ROWS.
TITLE PAGES, ii AND iii: EARLY MORNING LIGHT HIGHLIGHTS VINE LEAVES ALONG A WINDING ROAD IN THE SANTA YNEZ VALLEY.
(ALL OF ABOVE PHOTOS BY KIRK IRWIN.)

CONTENTS

❧ COOLING SUMMER FOG AIDS VINE GROWTH IN THE INLAND VALLEYS OF SANTA BARBARA COUNTY.

WINE AGES IN BARRELS AT RANCHO SISQUOC WINERY.

✏ BARRELS LINE A COLORFUL WALL AT BYRON WINERY.

INTRODUCTION

*T*he Santa Barbara-bound plane began its descent somewhere over Santa Maria on a warm, clear, September morning in 1965. The newcomer to Santa Barbara sat in a window seat, watching the land pass below and noticing patches of cultivated crops alternating with the typical brown hills and live oaks of the California summer countryside.

That evening at dinner, enjoying a bottle of Napa Valley Sauvignon Blanc, the new arrival—the senior author of this book—asked a Santa Barbara resident why they were not drinking local wines.

"Local wine? Grapes don't grow here," he said.

"Why not?"

"Well, I don't know," was the tentative answer. "Too dry, probably, or too far south. I don't know. But you have to get your wine from the Bay Area."[1]

❧ MANY SANTA BARBARA COUNTY VINEYARDS THRIVE AMONG OAK-STUDDED ROLLING HILLS.

*I*n the mid-1960s, few people in Santa Barbara knew that commercial grapevines were being planted in the Santa Maria and Santa Ynez valleys to the north. These new grape plantings marked the beginning of a rebirth of Santa Barbara County's wine industry, which had begun to flourish early in the century and shriveled during Prohibition. From modest beginnings that had grown only to 171 acres in 1970, vineyard acreage in Santa Barbara County climbed rapidly to nearly 4,800 acres in 1973 and then doubled to 9,500 acres by 1992.[2] Today grapes are the county's third-ranked agricultural product, surpassing avocados and lettuce and rivaling the county's top-earning crops—strawberries and broccoli.

By the end of 1996, the county's wine industry consisted of 50 growers who produced 39,138 tons of grapes with a market value of $51.6 million. In that year, wine sales brought an additional $69.2 million in gross receipts to

Santa Barbara wineries, which in turn spent over $26 million locally for payroll, taxes, promotions, and other goods.[3] In the short space of 30 years, a major industry had grown out of the region's soil and the imagination and labor of longtime residents and recent migrants.

*W*here would today's visitor find Santa Barbara County's wineries and vineyards? Without even leaving downtown Santa Barbara you can visit tasting rooms, sampling premium wines and getting a taste of what the county has to offer. To visit the vineyards and the wineries nestled among them, however, requires a short trip to the North County's ranching and agricultural region. (See pages 62-63 for detailed maps of the county's wine country.)

Santa Barbara County is a large quadrangle of rugged mountains that are stacked highest in the east and generally run westward toward the coast. Heavy winter rains over millions of years have cut two main river valleys where the ridges were softened and soil was deposited in bottomlands. On the south-facing coast, the rains created small flood plains where the creeks made their short run to the sea. Along these few waterways there was good land for agriculture. Spanish and Yankee settlers, calling upon their agricultural heritages, found some room to farm on the narrow south-facing coastal shelf where the city of Santa Barbara now sits. Yet today you do not find the county's vineyards along the coastline; only small patches of row crops and avocado and citrus groves are wedged into the narrow coastal shelf. To reach the grape-growing country, you must drive up Highway 101 from Santa Barbara along the county's south coast, then turn sharply inland to cross the Santa Ynez range at Gaviota Pass.

Descending the curves of the highway north of Gaviota you encounter the North County's farmland—the bottomlands and surrounding hills that Santa Barbarans are referring to when they say they are going "over to the valley." This is Santa Ynez Valley, one of three valleys in North County where the wine industry has flourished. Coming from Santa Barbara, it is the first and southernmost valley, cut east to west by the Santa Ynez River. As you continue north on Highway 101, the next center of grape-growing is the little Los

Alamos Valley. A number of small, ephemeral streams converge at Los Alamos Valley, which drains to the west in San Antonio Creek. From Los Alamos Valley, a low range slopes northward and then drops off to the Santa Maria River. This river has deposited a large agricultural plain, the Santa Maria Valley, on its way westward to the Pacific.

These three east-west trending valleys create the pattern of North County vineyards. Approaching Buellton, where Highway 246 crosses U.S. 101, you reach the base of a lopsided triangle that frames the county's vineyards and wineries. Few of the North County's other agricultural products—strawberries, broccoli, alfalfa, or lettuce—are planted in this hilly grape triangle, which sits back several miles from the sea. These other crops prefer lower land and thus are often visible from U.S. 101, while most of the grapes are not.

The premium wine grape was planted by a different logic. The grapevine likes well-drained soils and does not want its roots to stand in water. The vines yield poor wine grapes if they are situated too close to the ocean's cold onshore fogs or to the hot upper reaches of the river valleys. Vineyards are best located where the elevation and inland position combine to produce the right blend of cooling fog and solar warmth; in Santa Barbara County, this occurs at elevations ranging from 200 to 1,500 feet. — 3,200' for Barnwood

This is the Santa Barbara County wine country. Out of sight and mostly east of U.S. 101, the area is served by two-lane roads threading their way up the canyons and along the ridges. Once off the main highway, travellers do not see a single billboard, and Los Angeles seems much more than two hours away. The return leg of the triangle, however, is travelled southbound on Highway 101, with vineyards on both sides of the road for a time near the picturesque town of Los Alamos.

Today, just three decades since our traveller was told that "grapes don't grow here," visitors can enjoy Santa Barbara County's garland of vineyards. Much of the yearly harvest is transformed locally into wines of more than 40 labels, and the remaining grapes are eagerly purchased by wineries in the north. A $100 million wine and grape industry—a unique blend of farming and sophisticated craftsmanship—has forged a place for itself in the county economy and built a worldwide reputation as a producer of top-rated premium wines. ❧

❧ TRELLISING WEAVES INTRICATE PATTERNS IN A VINEYARD LANDSCAPE.

Chapter One

FROM THE MISSIONS TO PROHIBITION

During the seventeenth and eighteenth centuries, European migrants to the colonies on the east coast of North America had searched for an American Garden of Eden for grapes of wine quality, experimenting from New England through Virginia to Florida. Most of these grape-farming, winemaking ventures ended in frustration and defeat, although there were some modestly encouraging commercial successes in upper New York, along the Ohio River, and in Missouri. (See Appendices.) In hindsight, wine-appreciating Europeans—now Americans—were searching their way to California. The Spanish friars beat them there, however, coming up from Mexico on a religious and civilizing mission.

Spanish explorers found several species of wild grapes along the coast of California, but the fruit was small, seedy, and sour. The wine grape of today— *vitis vinifera*—is not indigenous to the state. Wine was unknown among all the native peoples of the Americas, including the Chumash of the Santa Barbara region. Grapes and wine were brought to California by Spanish explorers and Catholic priests in the late eighteenth century when the area was in fact a remote northern part of Mexico. (See Appendices.)

Santa Barbara County's three missions—Santa Barbara, La Purísima Concepción, and Santa Inés—were part of a string of 21 missions founded along the coast of Alta California between 1769 and 1823. Vineyards were planted around each mission within a decade of its founding, and the grapes

~ THE OAK-DOTTED RANCHLANDS THAT SURROUND MANY VINEYARDS IN SANTA BARBARA COUNTY HAVE CHANGED LITTLE SINCE THE MISSION ERA.

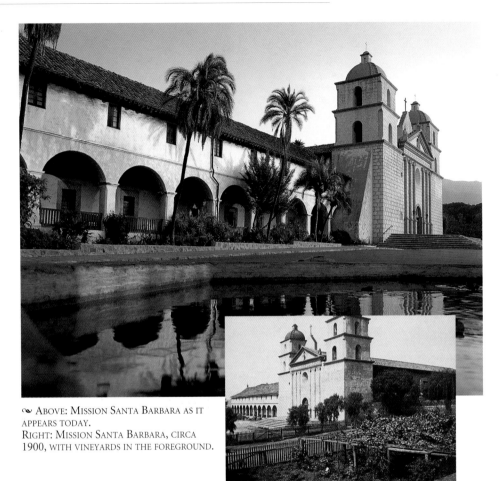

falling upon the grapes, and their hands were covered with cloth for wiping off the sweat, and each one was provided with a pole so that they could sustain their balance and not fall. The juice that ran off the hides was caught in some jars which were placed at the lowest point for that purpose. When these were full the juice was poured into a large wooden cask which served as a tank.[2]

The wine was fermented in wooden vats built by mission coopers, who later developed crude wine presses to replace the trampling of Indian feet. The Mission grape was unsophisticated in flavor, and produced a sweet, low-acid wine that fully met the needs of the sacrament. Wine was a secular pleasure as well, and the grape also could be turned into a brandy— *aguardiente*—which was easier to make and preserve than wine.

PLANTING VINES: SANTA BARBARA'S EARLY HERITAGE

Mission grapes thrived in California's warm climate, producing a sweet but vigorous table wine that kept well under adverse conditions. While mission-era wines were not known for their appeal to refined palates, at least one critic pointed to their high quality. Sir George Simpson, who visited California for the Hudson's Bay Company in 1842, recorded a favorable impression of Santa Barbara's creations:

∾ ABOVE: MISSION SANTA BARBARA AS IT APPEARS TODAY.
RIGHT: MISSION SANTA BARBARA, CIRCA 1900, WITH VINEYARDS IN THE FOREGROUND.

were pressed for sacramental wine. The region's native Chumash, compelled to live on mission land as a work force and wards of the Church, introduced the Europeans to many local plants, but there were no native grapevines of wine quality. The rootstock of *vitis vinifera* was brought to California by Father Junípero Serra around 1782, along with knowledge of winemaking.[1] California's wine story

began there, with a crude process described by Carlos Hejar in the 1830s:

They piled the grapes on a piece of sloping ground covered with well cleaned steer hides, then placed a number of naked, very well bathed Indians on the pile of grapes to trample them. The only clothing these Indians wore was a very thin loin cloth. They had their heads covered to prevent their hair

Most of the stuff which we had tasted, we should have carried away without compunction, thinking we were doing the owners a service; but we were sorry to deprive the very reverend donor, in the present state of his cellar, of a really good article.[3]

Even among the earliest of California winemaking efforts, then, Santa Barbara County's products were notable.

Wine grapes were planted as early as 1799, and with nearly 12,000 vines flourishing when a count was taken in 1843, Mission Santa Barbara was the first and largest grape-grower among the county's missions.[4] An 1854 map names three Mission Santa Barbara vineyards: San Jose, Vina Aroya, and La Cieneguita. Although dwarfed by the wines from 164,000 vines at Mission San Gabriel near Pasadena, Mission Santa Barbara's wine production ranked second among all California missions, with the largest local vineyard providing grapes for 6,000 gallons of wine a year.[5]

The scattered vineyards for all three missions in Santa Barbara County suggest broad experimentation for finding the best grape-growing locations. A plat of mission orchards and vineyards from 1854 reveals two La Purísima vineyards outside Lompoc, including a 17-acre planting on the road between San Julian Ranch and Jalama Beach.[6] Mission Santa Inés had a rather unsuccessful vineyard near the settlement itself, with other vineyards planted at Refugio, Tajiguas, and Arroyo Hondo.[7]

The mission fathers did not long hold a monopoly on vineyards or winemaking. In the late eighteenth century Santa Barbara became the site of one of the three Spanish presidios, or forts, in Alta California. Comandante Felipe de Goycoechea, who served as head of the Presidio de Santa Barbara from 1784 to 1802, established a vineyard in the area now bounded by Carrillo, Anapamu, Castillo, and De la Vina streets. (De la Vina Street earned its name from this early planting.)[8] Jose Antonio de la Guerra y Noriega, comandante of the Presidio from 1815 to 1846, also made wine, and it is estimated that he had 6,000 gallons on hand in 1860. He probably received winemaking assistance from his neighbor, Don Gaspar de Orena, who lived in a small adobe that you can still visit in downtown Santa Barbara on De la Guerra Street. Don Gaspar also made his own wine, and his son continued to produce wine at the family's small winery until the early twentieth century.[9]

Santa Barbarans hoped that vineyards would flourish all along the coastal shelf. In the city of Santa Barbara itself, close to the sea and seasonal fog, many vineyards were established. In 1794, the land grant for Rancho Nuestra Senora del Refugio provided the family of Jose Francisco Ortega with six leagues of land west of Santa Barbara, and Governor Diego

∾ THE SANTA INÉS MISSION FATHERS ESTABLISHED SEVERAL VINEYARDS IN THE SANTA YNEZ VALLEY DURING THE SECOND HALF OF THE NINETEENTH CENTURY.

Borica ordered that grapes be planted at the mouth of Refugio Canyon.[10] On Rancho Dos Pueblos, west of what is now the city of Santa Barbara, Nicholas Den tended 40 acres of vines by 1860. Over the mountains, vineyards were noted on Rancho Cañada de los Pinos (now known as the College Ranch) near the town of Santa Ynez on the stagecoach route, and vines were also planted along Zaca Creek north of Mission Santa Inés and on the Rancho Corral de Cuati.[11]

∾ THE VALLEYS IN NORTHERN SANTA BARBARA COUNTY ENJOY IDEAL GRAPE-GROWING CONDITIONS, WITH HOT DAYS TEMPERED BY COOLING OCEAN FOG.

During the first half of the nineteenth century settlers in the Santa Barbara region had developed many small vineyards and wineries, experimenting in widely varying terrain. By the 1860 census, Santa Barbara ranked third among California's wine producing counties, making 10,550 gallons out of a state total of 246,448 gallons.[12]

GRAPES AND WINE IN CALIFORNIA: TO 1880

Although vineyards were scattered about northern Santa Barbara County, the Los Angeles basin dominated the early California wine industry, producing over 150,000 of the nearly quarter million gallon output of wine estimated for 1860. But while Mission San Gabriel was the queen of mission winemakers, at El Aliso Ranch near what is now Union Station in Los Angeles, French immigrant Jean Louis Vignes, from a Bordeaux barrel-making family, established a commercial winery as early as 1833. Vignes was apparently the first to move beyond the Mission grape and experiment with cuttings of vines from France.[13]

After the Mexican War, ownership of California passed from Mexico to the United States, and gold fever brought thousands of newcomers to California. It has often been said that the real fortunes of the Gold Rush were made by the merchants who supplied the new migrants. In San Francisco, the new wine dealership of Kohler and Frohling tapped into a rising market. Since winemaking and grape-growing were centered in Southern California, the firm purchased vineyards in Los Angeles and produced commercial wines there, with vines tended by German farmers. Ultimately Kohler and Frohling's vineyards yielded 70,000 gallons a

year for commercial sale.[14] Production from this and other vineyards made Los Angeles the wine capital of the West.

Thus, on the eve of the Civil War, it was reasonable to expect Southern California to continue its pioneering role in American winemaking. Yet those who held that expectation would be proven wrong. Energy, capital, and innovation in the wine industry were even then shifting to the northern part of the state. The Gold Rush of 1849 and the resulting boom drew a growing mining population to the Sierra foothills, stimulating population growth in the port city of San Francisco and the state capital at Sacramento. With this surge of economic development, agricultural expansion inevitably included a search for "wine country" in the northern parts of the state.

The search was spurred by disasters to the south. A devastating attack of "Anaheim disease," an insect-borne bacterial infection, wiped out entire vineyards and crippled the Los Angeles-based wine industry in the 1880s. But the underlying problem for Southern California winemakers was that the region's large, red Mission grapes and warm climate typically produced very sweet fruit, yielding some notable port, sherry, and brandy but few respected dry table wines.[15] Viticulture would continue in Southern California, but mostly as a source of table fruit and raisins with

Santa Barbara's Famous Grapevines

*T*wo enormous vines growing near Santa Barbara in the late 1800s were early harbingers that the county's climate was well-suited for viticulture. The first was La Parra Grande, a vine planted in Montecito circa 1780 by Maria Marcelina Feliz. As the most popular story goes, Marcelina lived in Los Angeles with her family and was in love with José Dominguez, of whom her family did not approve. To save her from making a poor choice in marriage, her family moved to Montecito. Before they left, José begged Marcelina to wait two years before marrying another, and gave her the grape cutting as a reminder of his love. After two years, Marcelina was due to marry a man chosen by her family. On the eve of the wedding, however, José reappeared and won the approval of his beloved's family, having made his fortune mining gold.

La Parra Grande thrived on the Montecito property for about 86 years. The massive vine was said to produce at least four tons of grapes each year. A well-known landmark, it served the community as a meeting place and venue for local celebrations. By 1876, however, the vine was diseased and dying, and new owners of the property agreed to cut it down so it could be exhibited at the Philadelphia Exposition.

While the story of Montecito's famous grapevine is no doubt clouded by romantic elaboration, the history of its counterpart in Carpinteria—La Vina Grande—is fairly well documented. A Mission variety grape, the vine was planted in 1842 by Joaquina Lugo de Ayala at her home between what is today Santa Monica Road and Cravens Lane. La Vina Grande grew rapidly over its nine-foot-tall trellis and soon covered half an acre, making it a natural location for public meetings and social events.

In 1893, Jacob Wilson, the owner of the property at the time, was offered $1,000 for the vine so it could be displayed at the Chicago World's Fair. Wilson refused and continued cultivating his massive grapevine. At its peak, with a trunk nearly 10 feet in circumference, the vine was producing 10 tons of fruit per year in bunches from 9 to 22 pounds apiece! La Vina Grande died in the mid-1920s, however, and lengths of its branches served as tourist attractions in various locations until they disintegrated about a decade later. Listed in the Guiness Book of World Records, La Vina Grande is still considered to be the largest grapevine on record.

∾ TOP: MARIA LOUISA DOMINGUEZ SITS BENEATH LA PARRA GRANDE ARBOR IN MONTECITO. BOTTOM: THE FAMOUS CARPINTERIA GRAPEVINE, LA VINA GRANDE, THRIVED FOR OVER HALF A CENTURY.

some grapes for after-dinner wines. The search for sites to plant and harvest "fine wine" grapes, however, moved northward.

A WINE INDUSTRY TAKES ROOT IN THE BAY AREA

*M*ost of California's terrain is unsuitable for growing grapes for premium dry wines. In many areas, the cool breezes and occasional fogs moving inland from the Pacific Ocean are met by mountain barriers running north-south along the coast; the coastal shelf is narrow and in places nonexistent. Redwood trees thrive on these coastal ledges, but grapes require more sun and space along with the sea's cooling influence. Behind these coastal ranges, two major rivers—the Sacramento and the San Joaquin—have cut the great Central Valley, which nourished an agricultural empire in the twentieth century—alfalfa, melons, cotton, and even table and raisin grapes. But experience with grape-growing suggested to aspiring California winemakers in the latter half of the nineteenth century that vines producing premium wine grapes would not thrive in the unrelenting, hot summers of the interior. California settlers eager to establish viniculture instinctively sought a Mediterranean moderation, where long growing seasons and lavish sunlight could be combined with the cooling influence of the Pacific. There,

grapes for fine table wines could be produced without the overripening effects of torpid summer days.

There are only four places along the 850-mile California coastline where cool ocean air can penetrate significant distances into the interior: through the Golden Gate and across San Francisco Bay where the Sacramento River reaches the Pacific; at Monterey Bay where the Salinas River finally breaks through to the sea; at the very foot of the north-south coastal range in Santa Barbara County where the mountains abruptly turn to run briefly almost east-west and allow the Santa Maria and Santa Ynez river valleys the unique privilege of an east-west transit; and finally, near Santa Monica where the coastal mountains

rapidly give way to the greater Los Angeles plain. It was there, on the plateaus east of Los Angeles, where grapes were planted by the first European settlers, who produced wines that were limited to sweeter varieties.

Where else to search for more hospitable wine country but northward, in those regions of the state where California heat and cool Pacific air were more favorably blended? Inevitably, at the end of the nineteenth century, Californians with the talent, resources, and determination to produce fine American wines to rival those of Europe gravitated not to Santa Barbara County or the Monterey area, where there were neither natural ports nor a substantial population, but to the

∾ THE SOUTHWARD VIEW FROM BUTTONWOOD FARM VINEYARD LOOKS OUT TOWARD THE EAST-WEST TRENDING SANTA YNEZ MOUNTAINS. THIS RANGE HELPS CREATE A CLIMATE THAT IS CONDUCIVE TO WINE-GRAPE GROWING IN THE VALLEYS OF NORTHERN SANTA BARBARA COUNTY.

San Francisco Bay region, where ports and population centers were already well established.

California's Wine Boom

Vineyards were planted in every county of the Bay Area, with the greatest success experienced in Napa and Sonoma counties. An innovative cadre of European immigrants was drawn there, establishing vineyards and wineries whose products and names stake out much of the history of the California wine industry. Count Agoston Haraszthy, a dashing Hungarian political exile, founded Buena Vista Winery in Sonoma County in 1856. He toured Europe in 1861, returning to California with cuttings from 100,000 vines so experimentation could advance. In the 1860s and 1870s the great establishments of Napa and Sonoma counties took root, many of them carrying the European names of their founders—Beringer, Buena Vista, Italian Swiss Colony, Korbel, Schram, Charles Krug, Concannon.

The wine boom was unmistakable. In Santa Barbara County, the number of vines climbed from 15,000 in 1856 to 70,000 in 1857 and 90,000 in 1858.[16] Eager to promote and share in the credit for the growing industry, the California legislature excluded vineyards from taxation in 1859, commencing a long tradition of assistance to the enterprise

of winemaking. By 1862, the state government reported that California had eight times the number of grapevines it had in 1856.

Favorable tax status did not give the new industry clear sailing, however. California winemaking followed a roller-coaster pattern of surging production followed by severe reverses. Like all American farming in the late nineteenth century, vineyards and wineries were buffeted by the three depressions that flattened the national economy near the middle of

∾ Oak barrels have long been an integral part of the winemaking process.

each post-Civil War decade, bringing a cycle of boom followed by sudden overcapacity and falling prices.

Added to economic ups and downs were difficulties caused by agricultural pests. The dreaded root louse, phylloxera, favored California winemakers briefly in the 1860s by destroying virtually all vines in France, but then it turned upon California's vineyards in the 1870s.

(Records show that the louse skipped Santa Barbara County as it devastated Southern California vineyards in the 1890s.)[17] The industry's entrepreneurs were determined and resilient, however, replanting with phylloxera-resistant root stock and experimenting endlessly with new grafting.

Starting in the 1860s, there was help from government in the expensive business of research and dissemination of research results. In 1862 the federal government established the Department of Agriculture, and soon thereafter a system of land-grant universities. The University of California campus at Berkeley—where the viticulture and enology programs were founded—and later the new campus at Davis, became leaders in pioneering scientific agricultural methods. The spirit of innovation, long characteristic of winemaking, was especially intense in California. Another boost to the California wine industry occurred in the 1890s, when trade associations formed and thus centralized the spread of industry knowledge beyond what traditionally had been informal sharing between businesses.[18]

The state's adventure with wine advanced through the late nineteenth century and into the twentieth, despite difficulties associated with pests and the business cycle. Southern California's winemaking traditions continued, although increasingly eclipsed by the rising reputation of Bay Area wines. In the Cucamonga Valley east of Los Angeles, Secondo Guasti gambled on the future of wine in that region by establishing the Italian Vineyard Company, and San Bernardino's table grape, raisin, and sweet wine output kept more acres in vines there than in either Sonoma or Napa counties as late as the 1920s.

At the turn of the century, the major differences in the southern and northern branches of the state's wine industry lay first of all in the vine itself. In Santa Barbara County, the Mission grape held its ground, but in the Bay Area growers pursued a relentless search for new varietals. Entrepreneurial energy seemed clearly to flow to the San Francisco Bay region. By 1900 Sonoma County was home to at least 100 commercial wineries, and Napa Valley cradled thousands of acres of vines—mostly Zinfandel, Cabernet Sauvignon, White Riesling, Sylvaner, and Carignane. Napa led the state in wine

🌺 Santa Barbara's first major winery, La Bodega, was one of California's largest adobe structures when it was built in the 1860s.

output, with Sonoma second and Los Angeles third. And Bay Area wines were already being exported through San Francisco to the eastern United States, Asia, South America, and even wine-wise Europe.

Wine in Santa Barbara County: From Statehood to Prohibition

After the mission era, Santa Barbara County was settled by many people who thought wine a part of the good life. The area that is now downtown Santa Barbara contained a number of productive vineyards. In 1843 Felipe de Goycoechea, comandante at the Presidio de Santa Barbara, bought plants from French immigrant Pascual Botiller, who probably used the first wine press in the area. Botiller's winery survived until the 1890s. Another French immigrant, the consular representative Jules Goux, arrived in 1854 and maintained a store and small winery, while his relative Anastasio Goux ran a local hotel and saloon.[19]

Yankee immigrants also caught wine fever. Albert Packard planted an extensive vineyard on the west side of town in the late 1850s, and he built Santa Barbara's first major winery, La Bodega, on West Carrillo Street sometime after 1865. Standing two adobe stories high with a third wooden level above and a stone basement below, the structure—which some say was the largest adobe in California—had

🌺 The San Jose Winery in Goleta was built by the Santa Barbara Mission between 1824 and 1834.

walls three feet thick. Labeling wines under the "El Recedo" (The Corner) name, Packard made up to 90,000 gallons of wine annually and hired several professional winemakers, including one of the Gouxs of Bordeaux, whose "experience enables him to produce a finer grade of wines than can be made by those who have not made the business a life study." The specialty was a claret, "said to be the best variety that can be produced in California."[20] Prices for Packard's Santa Barbara vintages fetched up to twice that of Los Angeles area wines, and his wines sold in Los Angeles, San Luis Obispo, and as far away as Texas. At some point, probably in the 1880s, Packard's vineyard was destroyed by disease and wine grapes were replaced by olive groves. He left the city in 1887, and while the adobe winery survived the 1925 earthquake, it produced no wine after Prohibition.

In Goleta, the San Jose Winery, built by the Santa Barbara Mission between 1824 and 1834, was taken over by James McCaffrey, an Irishman lured to California by gold fever. McCaffrey maintained between 4,800 and 6,700 grapevines and continued the mission tradition of winemaking. After McCaffrey's death in 1900, Michele Cavaletto purchased the vineyard and continued to use its adobe winery for his vintages. Although Prohibition halted wine production, the winery still stands on the family's property, a county landmark whose adobe walls and tile roof protect a fermentation vat and winemaking materials.[21]

Others found their dreams of local wine production dashed. Colonel Russel Heath arrived in the Carpinteria Valley in the 1850s and accumulated 200 acres of land from impoverished Californio cattle ranchers during the droughts of the 1860s. Heath set out 10,000 grapevines and built a two-story winery equipped with a press, but south coast fog in Carpinteria brought mildew to his grapes.[22]

Despite these problems the area was still promising, and the Board of State Viticultural Commissioners' directory from 1860 recorded significant grape-growing and winemaking efforts in Santa Barbara County. Never on a scale to compete with the large vineyards that dominated the state's wine industry, the county's vineyards nevertheless managed to maintain a long-standing tradition. Although the center of California's wine industry began to move out of Southern

California by the latter part of the nineteenth century, at least 45 small vineyards of 1 to 40 acres persisted in Carpinteria, Santa Barbara, Goleta, Las Cruces, Lompoc, and Santa Ynez. With a total of 260 acres of wine grapevines (three-quarters of that acreage bearing fruit), Santa Barbara County had 17 winemakers. Most of the vineyards still grew Mission grapes, but a number had branched out into varietals including Zinfandel, Muscat, Olivet, and Tokay.[23]

❧ NEW LEAVES EMERGE ON THE VINES EACH SPRING.

In his 1888 study *California Pastoral*, historian Hubert Howe Bancroft noted that Mission Santa Barbara had been "famous for its choice wines and profuse hospitality."[24] In complimenting Santa Barbara's wines and terrain, Bancroft was not

alone among nineteenth-century observers. By the 1880s, when a new land rush came to California and the great ranchos of the south were subdivided, one promotional history commented of Ventura and Santa Barbara counties in grandiloquent style:

There are . . . not less than 400,000 acres of land which are capable of producing grapes of good quality. . . . The warm and protected valleys of the Santa Maria, Santa Inez and Santa Clara, with their lesser tributary valleys, with the sloping lands which surround them, form the natural home of the vine, and could, if occasion demanded, produce sufficient wine of a high quality to supply the utmost demands of commerce. In these sheltered and fruitful regions there is found, in the highest degree, the conditions for successful viniculture.[25]

The promotional local histories so popular in the late nineteenth century not only acclaimed the "perfect success" of grape growing in the Santa Barbara region, especially the North County, but commented:

It will probably not be long before some of the large ranchos of this district [Santa Ynez] will be subdivided and offered for sale. Rumor mentions La Zaca, Corral de Cuati, and Jonata Ranchos. . . . Experts in wine-making rank the Jonata and College Ranchos as first vine land. The soil and climate seem well adapted to grapes.[26]

This was a sound prophecy. The lands of the Jonata Rancho, on the north bank of the Santa Ynez River, and the College Rancho, near Refugio Road in Santa Ynez, today comprise some of the region's most prized vineyards. But in the 1880s the hope for a major wine industry in the county was premature.

OFFSHORE WINERY

The best-known and most successful Santa Barbara County vineyard and winery of the pre-Prohibition era was neither in the Santa Ynez Valley nor along the South Coast. It was the Santa Cruz Island Winery, established in the 1880s by French immigrant Justinian Caire and his family.

Santa Cruz Island, the largest of the county's Channel Islands, covers 96 square miles and is located 25 miles from the Santa Barbara Harbor. In 1869 it was sold to a group of ten directors of a San Francisco French bank, who created the Santa Cruz Island Company with plans to continue the development of the island as a ranch. Caire, a merchant and president of the group, owned the entire company and island by 1880 and set about creating a working farm. The island's main industry was sheep and cattle, and it became home to a small but busy community of workers. Caire himself supervised the building of a number of structures and a narrow-gauge railway running from the ranch warehouse to the wharf. Island vineyards were planted as early as 1884, in a period when California's

wine industry boomed due to the scourge of phylloxera in Europe. Zinfandel was the largest planting, but Caire was clearly no amateur, planting also Cabernet Franc, Cabernet Sauvignon, Barbera, "burgundy" (probably Pinot Noir), Grenache, Muscat, Riesling, Burger, Chasselas, and Sauvignon Vert. Vineyards filled the island's central valley, threatened only by the wild hogs who foraged during harvest season.[27]

European influence was strong on the island. Many of the ranch workers were recent Italian immigrants, and Caire himself knew well the founder of Italian Swiss Colony, Andrea Sbarboro,

☙ ABOVE, LEFT: WINE BARRELS READY FOR SHIPPING FROM SANTA CRUZ ISLAND TO THE MAINLAND. TOP: PETE OLIVARI PLOWING THE VINEYARD ON SANTA CRUZ ISLAND, EARLY 1900s. MIDDLE: SANTA CRUZ ISLAND WINERY, CIRCA 1937. BOTTOM: SANTA CRUZ ISLAND CHAPEL DEDICATION, 1891, AND SURROUNDING VINEYARDS, FIRST PLANTED IN 1884.

and his son-in-law, Pietro Rossi, who became president and general manager of that enterprise.

The island's first winery was a small wooden beekeeper's house, but Caire soon built a larger winery occupying two brick buildings made of island clay. Like other wineries of this era that lacked a cheap and reliable power source, Caire's relied on gravity flow, with the two buildings set on a slope. Winemaking went on in the higher building, and the wine cellar occupied the lower. Local resident George V. Castagnola recalled the island having "wonderful wine [and] wonderful grapes."[28]

Caire's winery and vineyards probably produced over 25,000 gallons per year in the 1890s. Production reached 44,000 gallons in 1904 and 83,000 gallons in 1910. By Prohibition, the island had about 150 acres of bearing vines. Island wines, mostly reds and dry, were sometimes purchased for blending. Caire sold his vintages to San Francisco and Los Angeles markets.

Thus the Santa Barbara region's wine tradition was small but promising as the nineteenth century ended. It consisted mostly of experimenting to find the right terrain, climate, and grape variety, conducted with the optimism found everywhere in the new Golden State. ✑

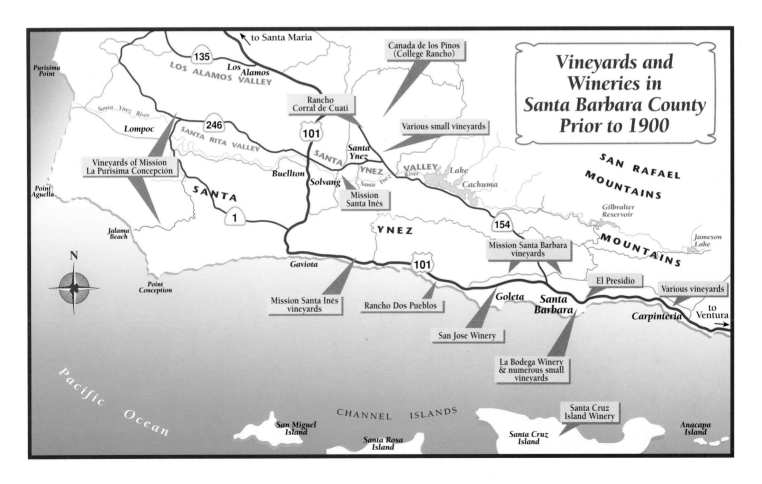

Vineyards and Wineries in Santa Barbara County Prior to 1900

Chapter Two

STRUGGLING BACK:
PROHIBITION TO THE 1960s

The future of the wine industry in California seemed bright as the twentieth century began. The Golden State's population was nearly 1.5 million, growing even more rapidly than the national population of 76 million. Per capita wine consumption in the United States was just over 0.3 gallons a year, low by European standards, but substantial enough to establish a national market for 50 million gallons of commercial wine by 1913.[1] Having produced more wine than any other state since 1870, by the turn of the century California had increased its share in the domestic wine market to 88 percent.[2] Its only serious rivals were European vintners, but many Americans sensed the new century might bring U.S. supremacy in all industries, including the production of wine.

There was one cloud on that horizon—the oddly named "temperance crusade" that was gaining strength everywhere in the nation after decades of agitation and political organizing. In Santa Barbara County, the 1874 founding of Lompoc as a "dry" town symbolized a national battle that was to be fought on many fronts.[3] Prohibitionist forces gained momentum at both the state and national levels during the pre-World War I progressive era, with seven states added to the dry list between 1907 and 1912. Hard liquor was the main target, but since wine contained alcohol, its use was also threatened by reformers. With American entry into World War I in 1917 came the final argument for nationwide Prohibition: Grain was needed to support armies and supply foreign markets deprived of French and German farm products, and it could not be

~ THE STAGE OF DEVELOPMENT WHEN RED GRAPES TURN THEIR ULTIMATE COLOR IS CALLED *VERASION*.

spared to make alcoholic beverages. After the Eighteenth Amendment was ratified in 1919 and Congress passed the Volstead Act in 1920 to enforce it, Prohibition was underway; the manufacture of alcoholic beverages for sale was outlawed in the United States.

LOMPOC WAS FOUNDED AS A TEMPERANCE COLONY IN 1874. ARTIST DAN SAWATSKY DEPICTS THIS ERA IN HIS 1991 LOMPOC MURAL.

With the onset of Prohibition, commercial winemaking had been banished and California's commercial sales of 50 million gallons of table wine simply disappeared. In Santa Barbara County, Caire's operation on Santa Cruz Island issued a last vintage in 1918, and Packard's downtown winery closed its doors. Yet somehow, California grape farming boomed throughout the 1920s, and wine

production and consumption steadily increased!

The unlikely increase in wine production was made possible by a loophole in the Volstead Act contained in Section 29. Created to calm the fears of vinegar and apple cider producers in the East, Section 29 allowed production of 200 gallons of "nonintoxicating cider and fruit juices exclusively for use in [the] home."[4] The ranks of home winemakers suddenly multiplied, many of them of French or Italian ancestry. Government agencies issued 45,000 permits to make vinegar as well as sacramental, flavoring, and "medicinal" wines, and the 200-gallon limit was dropped by administrative ruling in 1926. Officials interpreted these terms broadly, and soon there were commercial sales of these wines, often by phony priests, ministers, or rabbis. In 1928, California had a record 650,000 acres planted in grapes, many of them exported eastward where "home" winemakers stood ready for the crush. By the end of the decade, the state's wine production was estimated at 76 million gallons. Nationwide, per capita wine consumption had risen sharply in the 1920s, perhaps as much as 60 percent.[5]

While production increased, and well-known wineries such as Gallo and Christian Brothers got their start in the 1920s, Prohibition was, overall, a disaster for the state's winemakers, largely due to decreased wine quality.

Varietals intended for premium table wine found no place in the debased, mass markets of Prohibition, and those grapevines fell into disuse or were ripped out. In their place came thick-skinned varieties like Alicante Bouschet, which could survive shipping in rail cars to eastern cities. Thus, although the public consumed more wine, their selection was comprised of sweet, mislabeled, and crudely made impostors. California winemakers had slipped from the high standards they had achieved in the nineteenth century and faced a long uphill struggle to improve their product in order to rebuild the confidence and refine the tastes of the public.

THE GREAT DEPRESSION AND WORLD WAR II

With the repeal of Prohibition in December 1933—the fourth year of the Great Depression—California's now-legal wine industry was one of the few businesses that expanded. Since 1900, the nation's wine consumers had altered their tastes, from a two to one preference for dry wines at the turn of the century to a dessert or sweet wine preference of four to one by the time Prohibition ended—in part due to the lack of commercial dry wine production. Although a market for dry wine still existed, most commercial enterprises neglected this group of consumers in the belief that people still wanted the sweet, adulterated wines that had been available as "medicinal" or "sacramental" wine during the 1920s. Since the public was perceived as having permanently switched to sweet wines with high alcohol content, much of the industry's expansion came in the warmer Central Valley, which is well suited to growing sweeter grapes. There the number of bonded wineries doubled in 1933.

Even as it expanded, the state's wine industry was plagued by problems, including too many grapes, bad marketing and distribution methods, disorganization, and lack of capital. Further, when Prohibition ended, each state became responsible for its own laws on the distribution and taxation of wine, creating a chaotic market situation.[6] The quality of commercial wine was low and much of it was shipped in bulk, rather than being bottled where it was crushed, making it susceptible to tampering or adulteration by retailers or out-of-state bottlers.[7] Some of the potential market for finer table wines was retained by noncommercial family wineries that made a better product than could be bought in stores or bars. Indeed, as Robert Rossi of Italian Swiss Colony later declared, "Dry wine was actually ahead of sweet wine in total consumption, but more than two-thirds of the dry wine consumed was being made in basements."[8]

Some of these "basements" were in Santa Barbara County, where a substantial commercial wine industry had been built up before World War I and had never phased out completely, as many people had assumed. Bureau of Alcohol, Tobacco and Firearms (BATF) records at the University of California at Davis, along with interviews with descendants of local winemaking families, reveal that several bonded wineries continued to operate in Santa Barbara County at various times in the 1930s and 1940s. At Santa Barbara Winery—not to be confused with Pierre Lafond's present-day operation—grocer Manuel Jiménez sold wine from 1934 to 1937, if not longer. Ben Alfonso ran the Old Santa Ynez Winery from 1936 until the early 1940s, and customers were encouraged to bring in a jug for refills. The names of other individuals who held bonds to sell wine in the city of Santa Barbara in these years—Dardi, Piccioni, Boggio—reveal that Italian families, especially, carried on the commercial wine tradition, at least on the neighborhood scale.[9] Throughout the quiet years after Prohibition, the wine industry in Santa Barbara County apparently remained very much alive.

In the 1930s the state's commercial winemakers regrouped, and in 1934, some of the most famous names in the California wine industry joined to form the Wine Institute. The institute sought to increase national wine sales, establish industry standards for quality and production, and lobby

∾ TOP: OLD SANTA YNEZ WINERY LABEL, CIRCA 1936 - 1943.
BOTTOM: LENORE (MOORE) ALFONSO AND SON BENJIE POSE NEXT TO THE OLD SANTA YNEZ WINERY DELIVERY TRUCK, CIRCA 1940.

state and federal governments for industry assistance. In particular, they wanted governments to lower taxes on wine by reclassifying it as a food and not a spirit. California led the nation in reducing wine taxes and establishing uniform industry standards. Finding its other goals hard to achieve without further funding and authority, the Wine Institute in 1937 lobbied for the creation of a marketing order that forced state wine producers to contribute to a fund to be used to assist in promoting California wine. The result was the Wine Advisory Board, which focused attention on promoting the state's wine industry. Through an ambitious print campaign in popular magazines, the state's winemakers began to reach out to an audience of roughly 20 million Americans each week.[10]

With steps such as these, the industry groped toward recovery. World War II appeared to improve prospects even more. European wines were scarce, and the Depression-era shortage of capital had eased considerably. Large liquor companies in the East—Seagrams, Schenley, National Distillers, and others—made major investments in California vineyards, consolidating the industry and reducing the number of fringe players. These companies, however, lacked a knowledge of winemaking and the patience to rebuild the industry, so by mid-century California's wineries remained mostly in the hands of those with a ground-level commitment.[11]

A boom lay ahead in the 1950s and 1960s, although few foresaw it. One exception was wine writer and importer Frank Musselman Schoonmaker of New York, who as early as 1939 had added California wines to his trade. Perhaps he sensed the many layers of strength on which California winemakers could build.

THE YEARS OF REBIRTH: NAPA, SONOMA, AND THE BAY AREA

After the war, the U.S. wine industry was ripe for expansion and change. The sciences of grape-growing and winemaking—viticulture and viniculture—had expanded rapidly in the research programs and graduate education of University of California at Davis and Fresno State College (later University). These research centers worked in close collaboration with California's grape growers and winemakers, whose receptivity to new methods was enhanced by their lack of centuries-old European traditionalism. Wine writer Matt Kramer pointed out this advantage in predicting that the Golden State would surpass France:

Because of prohibition, no ingrained tradition presented resistance. The UC Davis enology and viticulture professors could fashion a new 'scientific' vision of how and where grapes should be grown and, even more important, how wine should be made.[12]

In addition, the state's wine industry, even prior to World War II, had organized itself internally to speak with one voice in promoting wine appreciation. California wineries, full of confidence, had virtually ended the practice of shipping the state's grapes east in boxcars or as juice, and were instead shipping them out in bottles with proud local labels.

More important, California by the 1960s had become the nation's trend-setter, and wine consumption was embedded in the message of Western good living. The California experience, whether to residents or tourists, included a trip to wine country. This focused attention on the wineries of Napa and Sonoma counties, where tourists, as tasters, were welcome to sample their premium, dry table wines and cocktail wines. Enormous vineyards in the Central Valley and South Bay counties, such as Livermore and Santa Clara, still produced grapes exported eastward as "jug" table wines, dessert wines, and sparkling wines.

Behind this increasing national attention to wine regions and their product were two basic trends: a gradually rising national consumption of wine and a shift in preference from sweet wines to drier wines. American wine consumption reached 100 million gallons by the mid-1940s and 145 million gallons by the mid-1950s, and by 1968, commercial dry wine consumption had outranked dessert wines. Sweet wine purchases had not decreased, but table wines, even with their higher price range, had surged ahead. Rising income levels were part of the explanation, but the appreciation of good wine was part of something larger that was taking place in American society—a more sophisticated, health-conscious, outdoor-oriented approach to life, which included consumption decisions.[13]

The economic, technological, legal, and social factors that promoted the development of California winemaking had come together after World War II and launched a remarkable era for the wine industry. As wine critic Hugh Johnson wrote:

Those first years of the '60s are the turning point in modern wine history. A radical new idea was born in many places at once; that wine was not an esoteric relic of ancient times that was disappearing even in Europe, nor just a cheap way to get drunk, but an expression of the earth that held potential pleasure and fascination for everyone.[14]

The enhanced status of wines, along with images of "wine country"—orderly rows of green vineyards set among browned, oak-studded hills, with the convivial tasting rooms and quaint towns that everybody knew to be in Napa Valley and Sonoma County—were also a powerful magnet for entrepreneurial people who

dreamed of a lifestyle that attractively combined the rural life of agriculture with the age-old art of making and marketing wine.

In 1963 UC Davis enologists identified Santa Barbara County as suitable for wine grapes. Today, more than 80 commercial vineyards are found in the county.

The efforts of California winemakers were eventually validated in 1976, when prominent French wine tasters conducted a blind wine tasting in Paris and judged two Napa Valley wines superior to their French rivals. The results shocked the French and changed the way the world perceived American wines.[15]

The dramatic postwar rise of the California wine industry to international prominence had its price. Land values surged upward in Napa, especially, but also in nearby Sonoma, limiting the region's ability to expand production as well as raising a formidable barrier for anyone seeking to start out there. If the California wine industry needed to expand, it would have to be elsewhere. But where?

Seeking an answer, many people turned to the research done on California climate and soils at UC Davis's enology program. In 1963, university enologists Maynard Amerine and Albert Winkler had designated Santa Barbara County as a Region I and II wine district suitable for the cultivation of premium varietal grapes—part of a I-to-V scale they had developed mapping California's best grape-growing regions (based on soil, water, and climate) and the likelihood of success of different varietals. The I and II rankings of Santa Barbara County, where no grapes grew at the time (or so people thought), indicated a cool region promising for varietals such as Chardonnay, Riesling, and Pinot Noir. Such studies pointed to expanding the industry southward, where coastal influence moderated the heat. History would have pointed in the same direction, but it had been forgotten.

Chapter Three

SANTA BARBARA COUNTY RENAISSANCE: 1960S-'70S

"The search for new places to grow grapes," in the words of the University of California's *Book of California Wine*, "now intensified. Places where vineyards had been planted but long forgotten were investigated...Temecula...the Salinas Valley...the Paso Robles area, the *Santa Maria area*, the *Santa Ynez Valley*...[Italics added]"[1] Southward, down the central coast toward that region where the mountains abruptly ran eastward and framed two hospitable river valleys—this was Santa Barbara County, one of wine's "places...long forgotten."[2]

Planting vines should come before winemaking, but in Santa Barbara County after World War II it seems to have been the other way around—at least on Mountain Drive, a winding, sometimes pot-holed road that runs for a considerable distance in the rugged foothills of the Santa Ynez Mountains above the city of Santa Barbara. In the '50s and '60s, there grew a community of small shacks and dwellings, pickup trucks, and an occasional chicken coop or tethered goat—a flourishing outpost of the hippie lifestyle. The "developer" was *bon vivant* and self-styled Renaissance man Bobby Hyde. Hyde bought a 50-acre parcel in the 1940s and began to sell smaller lots to young men and families he found compatible, including wine lovers Bill Neely, a potter and park ranger, and Frank Robinson, a local architect. The Mountain Drive culture embraced frequent festivals and parties, and wine was the river that ran through it all. Residents celebrated the spirit of Bacchus, and the year's main

~ THIS DAIRY BARN AT THE BETTENCOURT-DAVIDGE VINEYARDS NEAR SANTA YNEZ SERVED AS A WINERY IN THE EARLY DAYS OF THE MODERN WINE INDUSTRY OF SANTA BARBARA COUNTY.

event was an October grape stomp that began with a motorcade to San Luis Obispo County to pick up the required grapes. While destemming their fruit by hand, the "old goats" would then choose a Wine Queen.

∾ Mountain Drive Wine Queen, Rehlein Benedict, prepares to inaugurate the grape stomp, 1955.

It was her responsibility to inaugurate the stomp dressed in a gilded crown of grapevines and nothing else. The others joined in, without the crown.

"The way the wines were being made," confessed one participant, Stan Hill, "was too haphazard. It was a hell of a lot of fun—stomping around in the vat with a bunch of naked cuties didn't hurt—but it does-n't go terribly long into the process of making good wine."[3]

Bill Neely experimented on Mountain Drive's coastal hillsides with plantings of Folle Blanch, Semillon, Corbeau, and other cuttings from UC Davis's Department of Enology, but was defeated by fire, gophers, and rocky soils. Stan Hill claimed somewhat more success with Cabernet and Pinot Noir grapes. Both were discovering what history could have taught: the county's south coast was a good place to enjoy wine but a discouraging place to grow the grapes.

When Canadian-born architect Pierre Lafond opened a wine and cheese shop in the El Paseo district of the city, it soon became a gathering place for Mountain Drive residents. Urged on by his customers, Lafond created the Santa Barbara Winery in 1962, at first bottling and labeling wine brought from more northern counties, then in 1965 producing his own vintages from grapes shipped in from San Luis Obispo County.[4] It was the first commercial winery in Santa Barbara County since the 1920s, but it would not be the only one very long.

REPLANTING THE REGION'S WINE INDUSTRY

*U*nlike alfalfa, strawberries, and other annual row crops, grapes require substantial investment without immediate returns. New grapevines commonly take three to five years to produce their first crop, making prospective growers wary of untested growing areas. Anyone would be cautious about investing in a crop with a delayed return, especially in an area like Santa Barbara where the memory of earlier successes was no longer alive. Aspiring grape growers often turned to university scientists and viticultural professionals for advice before conducting their own site explorations and comparative studies. It must have lent encouragement to those exploring south of the Bay Area when UC Davis's Amerine and Winkler designated Santa Barbara County as a promising wine grape region.

Shortly thereafter, two UC Davis friends and former viticulture majors, Uriel Nielson and Bill DeMattei, began conducting field studies to discover promising new wine grape areas, even travelling to Europe to gain new insights. Nielson was not

Pierre Lafond in his Santa Barbara Winery in the early 1960s.

your average college student who appreciated wine. Having come from a family of grape growers in the San Joaquin Valley raisin industry, he was extending a family tradition. The choice the two friends made, after travel and study, was to buy land and plant vineyards in Santa Barbara County. The Santa Ynez Valley would be ideal, but land prices there were higher than in the Santa Maria Valley, and both valleys appeared to offer the loose, gravel-filled, well-drained soils compatible with grape growing. They bought approximately 100 acres east of Santa Maria on a portion of the old Rancho Tepusquet, and on that shelf north of the river planted 30 acres of grapes in 1964.

All the oldtimers agree that Nielson and DeMattei were the first to plant grapes in Santa Barbara County in the renaissance of the wine industry that began in the 1960s. After that, it becomes impossible to establish a rank order of who came next, and indeed some of those arriving a bit later may have dreamed of rooting the vine in Santa Barbara County soil even earlier than Nielson and DeMattei. More important than establishing who was first is recognizing that the growing demand for premium wine combined with the enticing image of a lifestyle that embraced both the honest labors of farming and the sophisticated mystique of wine drew a small but growing group of pioneers to replant an industry.

After four years of careful planting and pruning, Nielson and DeMattei harvested their first grapes in 1968. They had put in Cabernet Sauvignon, Sylvaner, Riesling, Chardonnay, and Sauvignon Blanc grapes, gambling across the red-white spectrum. Their gamble, however, was comfortably backed up by a friendly giant from the north. Brother Timothy and his colleagues at Christian Brothers in Napa Valley had encouraged the Santa Maria venture from the start, and when the grapes were ready for harvest in 1968, they offered a five-year contract paying $325 per ton. California grapes in those days seldom sold for more, even in Napa. Christian Brothers winemakers privately congratulated Nielson and DeMattei on the quality of their first crop, even though the reds would not be marketed as wine for four years. By the second harvest (1969), Brother Timothy even suggested that Santa Barbara County grapes were better than the Napa fruit, a broad, early judgment meant to be encouraging. And it was.

THE NIELSON VINEYARDS, NOW PART OF THE BYRON ESTATE VINEYARDS, ARE THE OLDEST COMMERCIAL GRAPEVINES IN SANTA BARBARA COUNTY.

On September 30, 1969, the *Santa Barbara News-Press* ran an article heralding the arrival of Santa Barbara County's "newest and perhaps most glamorous crop—winegrapes."[5] Shortly thereafter, Pacific Gas and Electric Company reprinted the article in pamphlet form and circulated it to agricultural customers. PG&E was happy to encourage any new industry that might increase population and electricity usage in rural North County. The utility's reprint brimmed with enthusiasm for the DeMattei-Nielson venture and quoted vineyard manager Bill Collins's confident prediction:

We've proved [Santa Barbara] is one of the rare places in the world where high-quality, dry, wine grapes can be grown. If a rancher said he was going to start a vineyard, he would find a winery representative at his door the next day offering a contract for his future production.[6]

The news of grape-growing success spread quickly. Discussions with DeMattei, Nielson, and growers from outside the county convinced Boyd and Claire Bettencourt to plant 15 acres of their "worst" Santa Ynez Valley land (i.e. too steep for any other kind of agriculture) in Cabernet vines in 1969. Encouraged to plunge in further by neighboring farmer G. Gifford Davidge, the Bettencourts made him a partner, liquidated their dairy herds, and planted more grapes. Agents from Paul Masson Winery of Soledad soon signed a contract paying nearly $800

per ton for their first harvest, expected in 1973. The sum was extraordinary, since the same varietals had been selling for around $350 a ton only five years earlier.[7] The crop was selling higher than the going market rate in the state, even before it was harvested.

Not surprisingly, others would soon follow the Bettencourts. The center of the action was east of Santa Maria, along the north (Tepusquet Mesa) and south banks of the Santa Maria River. Among this new, diverse group of grape growers was cattle rancher James Flood III, owner of the 37,000-acre Rancho Sisquoc whose northwestern corner touched the Santa Maria River. Flood had been

TOP: RANCHO SISQUOC'S ORIGINAL WINERY BUILDING NOW SERVES AS ITS TASTING ROOM. BOTTOM: HAROLD PFEIFFER, SHOWN IN A PHOTO TAKEN AT THE WINERY'S 25TH ANNIVERSARY CELEBRATION, PLANTED THE FIRST VINES AT RANCHO SISQUOC.

satisfied with cattle ranching until the early 1960s when he was encouraged by Almaden to consider planting vineyards to supply its Bay Area winery with grapes. This was "before DeMattei and Nielson got in here," remembers Harold Pfeiffer, who became Flood's ranch manager in 1963. Although Almaden changed ownership and nothing came of the discussions, Flood irrigated some of his acreage on the south bank of the river, and, as Pfeiffer recalled, "I saw these grapes being planted next door to us, over here," pointing north across the river to Tepusquet Mesa. "So I got a few clippings from them and in '68, '69, I planted them in a nursery. . . . The next year [1970], we either had to throw them away or do something with them, so we decided to start planting a vineyard."

Rancho Sisquoc put in about 30 acres of Cabernet Sauvignon and Johannisberg Riesling, and expanded the plantings slowly. Who knew if they were growing the right varietals in the right places? The talent pool was small. "I remember we used to have our meetings," said Pfeiffer. "We'd get together for lunch, and there'd be three of us there." The three were Pfeiffer, DeMattei, and Bob Woods, manager of the Suey Ranch who planted 25 acres in Pinot Noir north of the river in 1969. "We were the grape industry."[8]

This recollection captures the pioneering aspect of the early grape planters in the county, but overstates their isolation. The Suey Ranch plantings were selected with the help of the established Napa Mirassou family as well as experts at UC Davis. Bob Woods knew nothing about grapes, and at that time "had never had a glass of wine in my life." Stephan Bedford, former Rancho Sisquoc winemaker now in partnership with grower David Thompson at Bedford Thompson Winery and Vineyard, has interviewed the planters of the 1960s and reports that they "did a lot of research" and received advice from the Bay Area's Robert Mondavi, Brother Timothy, and famed wine expert André Tchelistcheff. In the end, of course, the advice came down to their own instincts: "Do it or don't do it."[9]

Across from Rancho Sisquoc on the north bank of the Santa Maria River, grape growers DeMattei and Nielson soon had company. The Suey Ranch plantings were small, a cautious local experiment. But 1969 also brought another scout who, like Nielson, came from another established grape-growing family. This was Louis Lucas, from the Lucas family, who managed San Joaquin Valley table grape acreage from a base in Bakersfield. Lucas, who knew both DeMattei and Nielson, was eager to branch out from his family's table grape business, and he liked good wines. Joined by his brother George, Louis Lucas quickly learned of the Nielson-DeMattei venture near Santa Maria, visited the site, and then travelled to Napa to visit Brother Timothy at Christian Brothers "to try to pin him down on how good or how bad the grapes were. I promised him I would never tell, but he did say the grapes were decent and that he would consider paying Napa Valley prices for them. That really got me charged up."[10]

❧ Top: Louis Lucas, at right, in Tepusquet vineyard in the early 1970s.
Bottom: Bob Woods has grown grapes at Rancho Vinedo since 1973.

☙ DALE HAMPTON, SHOWN IN A 1997 PHOTO, HAS BEEN AN INNOVATIVE GROWER AND VINEYARD MANAGER IN THE COUNTY SINCE THE LATE 1960s.

Louis and George, with the help of their high school classmate Dale Hampton—a manager on his own family's land—"looked at soils, water, temperature conditions, [and] frost threat conditions," and began seeking the capital required to plant a crop that would not go to market for three to five years. Hampton spent a year doing research for a site, starting in Napa but quickly looking southward, and in 1969 he settled on Tepusquet Mesa. The Lucases bought 1,300 acres there—calling it Tepusquet Vineyard (to the irritation of some others growing grapes on the mesa)—and sent Hampton to manage it. There was much to learn about grape growing in the new region, and Hampton, who formed his own management and consulting firm in 1972, would be a central figure in the learning and

teaching. "Nobody was sure what they were doing," Louis Lucas conceded years later. "We took the advice of a winery and we planted mostly reds, and we should have been planting whites. Things like that." Added Hampton, "The pioneering was still pioneering."[11]

Although the Lucas brothers, Hampton, and Nielson all came from table grape-growing families, and Nielson and DeMattei had studied viticulture at UC Davis, they had much to learn about growing wine grapes, especially in Santa Barbara County where the history of grapes and wines was virtually forgotten. By trial and error supported by science, the farmers who launched the rebirth of the industry had to learn how, where, and which varietals of wine grapes to cultivate. Dale Hampton was a relentless experimenter, and was backed by Lucas family capital. He travelled to Napa "to learn by their mistakes," as he put it, especially in the start-up decisions about water systems, vineyard stakes, and trellises. Hampton was soon innovating by planting a special, virus-resistant "super clone" instead of ordinary clippings that would have cost half the price, then adding further to the initial cost by choosing metal instead of wooden stakes. Healthy plants and bountiful early yields at Tepusquet Vineyard

were encouraging, but Hampton the veteran farmer knew what lay ahead—birds, gophers, frost, disease, and replanting or grafting where they had made mistakes in choosing varietals or when the market shifted.[12]

Some of the early grape planters did not know these things in advance, for they had no farming background at all and started farther back on the learning curve. Lompoc dentist Bill Mosby and his wife Geraldine planted their first wine grapes in 1971 on eight acres of farmland on the north bank of the Santa Ynez River, after discussing their plans with an old pro, former college fraternity brother Robert Gallo.[13]

That same year two more non-farmers completed their studies of the best place for grapes in California and

☙ LEFT TO RIGHT, BILL MOSBY AND SONS MIKE AND GARY, 1972, IN THE FAMILY'S YEAR-OLD VINEYARD NEAR THE SANTA YNEZ RIVER OUTSIDE BUELLTON. BOTH SONS CONTINUED IN THE WINE BUSINESS, MIKE AS A GROWER AND GARY AS A WINEMAKER (CHIMÈRE WINERY).

selected a 700-acre bean and cattle ranch just west of the Mosby property. Geographer Richard Sanford and botanist Michael Benedict had discovered they loved wines more than their jobs at UC Santa Barbara, and two years of research in France and California led them to the site across and downriver from the Mosbys. Like others putting in the first vines in the county, Sanford and Benedict were venturing beyond their knowledge, experience, and capital resources. "It was an outrageous thing to be doing—starting from scratch," Sanford admitted years later.

All the early planters were in some degree starting from scratch, since the region was a blank page even to the Lucases and Dale Hampton. But while others saw themselves as growing grapes, Sanford and Benedict started with the intention of making wine, becoming grape growers as a means to an end rather than as an end in itself. "I decided that agriculture was the route I wanted to take [to winemaking]," Sanford recalled. "The whole vertical integration . . . the fact that we would have control over all of the phases [of our business] was most unusual and appealing." They planted 100 acres over two years in Chardonnay, Pinot Noir, White Riesling, Cabernet Sauvignon, and Merlot. The ranch had no electricity, so while waiting for the grapes to mature, Sanford read books on viticulture by gas lights. Benedict hoped

they had found a niche where the coastal fogs pushed away the frost and grapes could thrive.[14]

FROM VITICULTURE TO VINICULTURE

While aspiring new grape farmers were launching personal ventures that grew out of family tradition or a graduate student's dream, to landowners and real estate people in the area, the 1970s North County wine boom was a new and entirely welcome pressure for "development"—investment in land and equipment, rising land prices. Suddenly it became important, if you owned land, to have an opinion about where grapes should and could be planted.

In 1971 Dean Brown, rancher and real estate investor, decided to sell his Corral de Cuati ranch. He utilized the real estate expertise of Richard Dick and T. Hayer, who in turn hired the California Farm Management consulting firm to investigate the ranch's possible agricultural uses. The area's grape-growing potential—enhanced by successes in the area, UC Davis's studies, the PG&E Report, and Bank of America studies—provided fuel for sales pitches.

Leonard Firestone, Ambassador to Belgium and owner of Firestone Tire and Rubber Company, purchased 2,850 acres of the ranch.[15] It was not long before his son, A. Brooks Firestone, showed an interest in the

☙ BROOKS FIRESTONE AND SON ADAM (WHO BECAME WINERY PRESIDENT IN 1995), AT LEFT, STAND IN FRONT OF WINERY BUILDING SITE IN 1975. WINEMAKER ANTHONY AUSTIN IS AT FAR RIGHT.

property. No longer enthusiastic with his executive role with the family firm, Brooks Firestone left the corporation's London office and moved his family to the ranch, located just north of Los Olivos. Soon he announced plans for a 300-acre vineyard of premium varietal grapes intended for the market— which meant the large wineries based in Napa and Sonoma. There was no initial intention to make wine.

The expansion of grape acreage in Santa Barbara County owed a good bit to the boosterism of Bank of America. The bank's report on the outlook for wine predicted that changing national tastes and rising affluence would lead to an ever-escalating demand for grapes, and its 1973 *California Wine Outlook* forecast that the 10 to 13 percent growth rates in wine consumption experienced from 1969 to 1973 would continue into the future. Other authorities were equally optimistic. "California is experiencing a grape rush bigger than the gold rush of 1849-50," reported none other than Leon D. Adams, the foremost wine writer who in the 1930s had cofounded both the Wine Institute and the Wine Advisory Board.[16]

The first years of the 1970s were indeed encouraging to local planters and those who watched their progress. After Christian Brothers's enthusiasm for DeMattei-Nielson grapes, it did not escape notice that Rancho Sisquoc signed a six-year contract with Geyser Peak Winery in 1974. The region's press began to tout the grape future of the county, and industry journal *Wines and Vines* in 1971 announced a "Miracle at Tepusquet."[17] By 1972 Mary Vigoroso, the self-proclaimed "Ol' Winemaker," established a 350-acre vineyard in Los Alamos and began production of 800 cases of wine under the Los Alamos Winery and Hale Cellars labels.

In this optimistic climate, more vines went into Santa Barbara County

SANTA BARBARA WINERY'S LAFOND VINEYARD, PLANTED IN 1972, IS ON THE SANTA YNEZ RIVER WEST OF BUELLTON (SANTA RITA HILLS IN THE BACKGROUND).

Bien Nacido Vineyard

*T*oday the Santa Maria Mesa is blanketed by vines, including hundreds of acres at Bien Nacido Vineyards. A much smaller planting of Mission grapes existed 150 years ago near the historic Tepusquet Adobe, which still stands at Bien Nacido.

Over the last 25 years, many winemakers have earned acclaim for wines made from Bien Nacido

TEPUSQUET ADOBE AT THE BIEN NACIDO VINEYARDS.

Pinot Noir, Chardonnay, Pinot Blanc, and Syrah. Plantings of new clones of these varieties plus Pinot Gris, Barbera, and Nebbiolo continue the tradition of viticultural experimentation on the mesa.

soil. "The wine market just took off," comments Pierre Lafond, who, when he could no longer find grapes to purchase for his urban Santa Barbara Winery, started his own vineyard west of Buellton in 1972. The DeMattei-Nielson and Tepusquet vineyards continued to expand almost yearly, and they soon had more company. Bob and Steve Miller bought the westernmost portion of Rancho Tepusquet and thought they had rights to the name, until the Lucas family adopted the name for their vineyard. The Millers still went ahead, planting without a vineyard name. As Bob Miller recalled: "In the fervor of the

grape plantings and the report by the Bank of America, we got caught up in it and in 1973 ended up planting 640 acres of grapes in Santa Maria." They hired Dale Hampton to put in the best trellising and water systems. "At that point people were just shaking their heads saying, 'My gosh, you should call it a Cadillac vineyard,'" Miller remembers. They decided on the name Bien Nacido, the Mexican expression for being born with a silver spoon in your mouth.[18]

By the end of 1972, Santa Barbara County was only a few years away from contributing substantial tonnage to the California grape market. Of the

1,894 acres of vines in the ground, only 120 acres were actually bearing fruit. Would the grapes be good enough to hold the high prices northern wineries initially offered? Would the market grow 10 percent a year forever, as Bank of America had implied? These were reasonable concerns among those who had staked out—literally—a commitment to the future of the wine grape, as well as those thinking of joining them.

A third concern began to emerge among those with a long view: was Santa Barbara County destined to remain a grape farm for Bay Area wineries? If local grapes were as good as climate-soil studies forecasted and early harvests hinted, why allow the grapes to disappear into the vats of Napa-Sonoma wineries, when Santa Barbara County might build a reputation of its own for superiority? But a regional identity could not be built if bottles of wine did not carry the Santa Barbara County designation in some fashion. One grower who saw the need to change the pattern of exporting all the region's grapes to northern wineries was Harold Pfeiffer of Rancho Sisquoc. Although James Flood's original intent at the ranch was simply to grow and sell grapes, Pfeiffer began making experimental wines "on a very small basis in 1972,

in a way to sort of promote that there can be quality wines made in this area," a colleague recalls.[19]

❧ A REBUILT BARN NEAR THE VINEYARD BECAME THE MOSBY WINERY AT VEGA VINEYARDS DURING THE GRAPE GLUT OF THE EARLY 1970S.

A move toward establishing more wineries began after this surge of vineyard planting. Building regional identity was one motive, as with Pfeiffer, who was thinking mostly of *grape* identity. Sanford and Benedict decided from the start to combine agriculture with the art of winemaking, more for

aesthetic and personal reasons than concerns for the region's best interests. For other early growers, adding a winery seemed a good business move as insurance against times when grapes didn't sell. "It became very evident to me," said Brooks Firestone, recalling the 1971-72 planning and launch-ing of Firestone Vineyard, "that too many people in California were putting in grapes." He went to his industrialist father and said, "Dad . . . you're a farmer, and the farmer always gets screwed. So perhaps it's better to make wine out of these grapes if indeed this research is correct" about their potential. Not far away, two other grape farmers had already arrived at the same conclusion. "We meant to sell grapes," recalled Jeri Mosby, but when they first had trouble in the grape mar-ket, the Mosbys concluded that "we could do better making wine" in that rebuilt red barn near the vineyard.[20]

Trouble selling grapes had come much sooner than even Firestone expected. Hindered by the oil embargo, a surge of inflation, and President Nixon's unsettling decision to float the dollar on international exchanges, the American economy slumped into a recession in the early 1970s, then experienced sluggish growth through the rest of the decade.

One result was that wine consumption did not continue the phenomenal increases experienced from 1969 to 1972. Growth in consumption slumped to 3.1 percent in 1973,

❧ The Tepusquet brand was created in 1975 when an oversupply of grapes forced local growers to become vintners.

although this amounted to a record marketing of 347 million gallons, of which California alone produced 241.8 million gallons.[21] In 1974, with 62,000 acres of vines bearing fruit for the first time, wine grape prices fell an average of $120 per ton statewide. Vineyard plantings had outpaced the market, which had suddenly dropped from double-digit annual growth to less than one percent growth in 1974.[22]

Suddenly Bank of America's 1973 prediction that national wine consumption would rise from 350 million gallons to 650 million gallons by 1980 seemed far too optimistic, as did the

report's words: "It is improbable that the economy of the United States will falter for any length of time between now and 1980."[23]

In retrospect, the 1973 Bank of America report "was overdone . . . way too optimistic. So it got a lot of people into grapes who shouldn't have been in the grape business," commented Dale Hampton. California growers had doubled the statewide acreage devoted to wine grapes between 1965 and 1973, farming a total of 266,000 acres. The contraction in wine demand that came with the recession quickly exposed the overexpansion in grape acreage, and the growers in Santa Barbara County, a relatively new grape region, were hard hit. In 1975 Beringer, uncomfortable in a five-year contract with Tepusquet while grape prices were rapidly falling, broke out of the contract, and "all of a sudden we have no home for the grapes," as Louis Lucas recalled. "We had all these grapes and no wineries, [so] we made wine . . . with a Tepusquet label and we made the wine at San Martin winery [near Gilroy]. Our biggest obstacle was trying to sell grapes from an unknown region." There were years when they couldn't even sell a crop and were forced to turn the grapes into what Lucas called "dago red" just to salvage something from the harvest. Los Alamos grape-grower Joe Carrari did the same with his surplus grapes, because in his words

"you can't make money just selling grapes to wineries."[24]

The slump in wine grape prices of the mid-1970s, along with the 1976 repeal of the favorable tax treatment for investment in vineyard acreage, slowed the pace of wine grape plantings statewide. These discouragements tempered but could not squelch the enthusiasm of those who believed in a bright future for the wine industry in general and in the potential of Santa Barbara County in particular—and who wanted to be part of the unique lifestyle associated with winemaking.

In 1975, the Bettencourt-Davidge partnership answered the grape glut by establishing the Santa Ynez Valley

❧ Fred Brander was winemaker at Santa Ynez Valley Winery before opening his own winery in 1979.

LEFT: RICK LONGORIA WAS WINEMAKER FOR J. CAREY CELLARS, THEN THE GAINEY VINEYARD, AND MADE WINE FOR HIS OWN LONGORIA LABEL AS WELL.
ABOVE: JOE CARRARI HAS GROWN GRAPES IN SANTA BARBARA COUNTY SINCE 1974 AND IS KNOWN FOR HIS DAGO RED WINE.

Winery where Refugio Road slopes toward the river east of Solvang. They crushed their first grapes the following year. UC Davis graduate Fred Brander signed on as first winemaker, and the winery's barrel-fermented Sauvignon Blanc, blended with Semillon, brought wide attention to the region's wines when it won a gold medal from the Los Angeles County Fair in 1977. It was "the first year we showed," remembered the late Boyd Bettencourt. "That was just like a high school kid going to win the Olympics, you know, little, teeny old winery down here, first year out and so forth, but we found later we could [win medals] pretty often with a good winemaker and quality grapes." Brander went on to establish his own winery in 1979 in a barn at the vineyard his family had planted in 1975 outside of Los Olivos.[25]

The Santa Ynez and Santa Maria valleys were indeed sprouting with new winemakers in the mid-1970s, with existing wineries serving as postgraduate schools for enologists and launching pads for additional wineries. Experiencing marketing difficulties, the Bettencourts took the lead in setting up Los Vineros in Santa Maria, a cooperative winery that for a time sold wines made by early planters Nielson and Woods, Eric Caldwell, Bill and Dean Davidge, George Ott, and Charlotte Young. Enthusiastic and undeterred by lack of experience, dentist Gene Hallock left a successful practice in 1974 and with his wife, Rosalie, moved an old-fashioned gas station from Santa Barbara to serve as headquarters for Ballard Canyon Winery near Los Olivos.[26] The Alamo Pintado Vineyards started by McDonnell-Douglas executive Jack McGowan in 1975 sold to Dr. J. Campbell Carey two years later, who in turn started J. Carey Cellars in a dairy barn and lured away Firestone's Rick Longoria as winemaker. Retired oil executive Marshall Ream planted a vineyard on a plateau near the headwaters of Zaca Creek, and in 1976 convinced recent Fresno State University enology graduate Byron

(Ken) Brown to be the first winemaker at his Zaca Mesa Winery. Brown had intended "to stay at best three years here . . . and make my mistakes on somebody else's money" before heading for Napa. He never migrated farther than the north edge of Santa Barbara County, however, going on to establish Byron Vineyard and Winery after his years at Zaca Mesa.

Looking back, Kate Firestone, wife and business partner of Brooks Firestone, was right. A lot of people "started dreaming back in the early seventies or late sixties" about starting a small winery, and by the mid-1970s they were ready to move. More local wineries were a welcome corrective to the industry's early structure, which had been over-whelmingly tilted toward agriculture. As late as 1975, 32 growers of commercial wine grapes tended 3,864 acres in the county, but there were only four vintners, and the largest of these—Firestone—had yet to market its product. A decade later, 16 wine-makers were bottling wines from nearly 10,000 acres of county vines.[27]

The trend seemed to indicate a better balance in the region between viticulture and viniculture, sometimes separate activities that flourish best in close proximity. The area's growers needed successful regional wineries to provide a more stable market, and throughout the 1970s several vineyard owners established wineries, vertically integrating their businesses. People whose main goal was winemaking in the first place were sometimes starting up in rebuilt farm buildings or in warehouses, but often they saw the logic of vertical integration back into agriculture, despite its unusual demands and risks. Said UC Davis's A. J. Winkler, "If you don't control the grapes, you can't consistently make a quality wine, because sooner or later somebody's going to buy those grapes out from under you."[28]

Winkler's remark might have been reversed: If you are going to grow and sell quality grapes, you've got to have excellent wineries building the region's reputation. In Santa Barbara County in the 1970s, it appeared that both versions were making converts. Wineries in or near their own vineyards were multiplying, whether the impulse came from the dedication to a way of life in grape growing or from the passion for winemaking. As the 1980s arrived, it could be seen that Santa Barbara County would not be only a grape farm for faraway producers.

Little else was clear, however. Were the grapes in the right place? In a "new" region (with no recorded viticultural history), only trial and error would bring the best marriage of wine and *terroir*—the French term for an area's terrain and climate. The grape glut of the mid-1970s prompted

∾ Zaca Mesa Winery occupies a rustic building fronted by vines along Foxen Canyon Road.

radical rethinking of earlier decisions, and by one estimate, 10 percent of the county's vineyard acreage in that decade was ripped out or regrafted.[29]

Experimentation is the rule rather than the exception in all winemaking, but especially in a newly opening region. How good were Santa Barbara County wines, now that they were entering the market and competing with the best premium wines?

There were early signs that the area's wineries might very quickly "make quality wines" out of the region's quality grapes. Wine writers Hugh Johnson and Bob Thompson wrote of the Santa Maria Valley in 1976:

Most of the awesomely fast development of a 5,000 acre vineyard district has taken place on benchland that looks south, in the European tradition. Climate regions I and II prevail in spite of the southerly latitude because the tail of the great coastal fog bank curls easily and regularly into the Santa Maria's valley. The southerly exposure and the frequent mists have caused some skilled observers to think that this might, just might, be the place in all of California for Pinot Noir. It'll take some years before anyone will know.[30]

Santa Barbara County wines began gaining recognition that very year, however, when *Los Angeles Times* wine writer Dan Berger reported that Sanford and Benedict's first Pinot Noir (1976) "was a wine of cult proportions, with wine collectors knocking themselves out to get a bottle."[31]

Pinot Noir was soon joined by other varietals in the awards circle. In the fall of 1978, Firestone winemaker Anthony Austin—trained at UC Davis and a protégé of André Tchelistcheff, the "Father of California viticulture"—produced a Chardonnay that won a Double Gold Medal in London, earning the first "world class" award for the county. And Zaca Mesa Winery began to win awards in California wine tastings with its first vintage in 1978, going on to receive state awards for each of the six varietals it produced in 1982.

Guidebooks and articles were another way to spread the word of the region's potential for high-quality premium table wines. While the 1970 edition of Bob Thompson's *Guide to California Wine Country* (Sunset) did not mention Santa Barbara, the 1977 edition noted briefly that "farther south, in Santa Barbara County, 6,000 acres of vines have been planted since 1971 and the Firestone family operates a pioneering winery." The 1979 version of Thompson's guide included a complete rewrite, and seven Santa Barbara County wineries were included. "From the viewpoint of visitors . . . there has been a tremendous revolution in the state's wineries since 1968," it concluded. In 1978, the *New York Times* ran a rather lengthy article on Firestone Vineyard in its "Sunday Magazine." Recognition of the Santa Barbara region was uneven, however. In Robert Balzer's *Wines of California*, published that same year, Santa Barbara County was not on the South Central Coast map, and only two regional wineries earned a fleeting mention.[32] There was still a long way to go. ∾

∾ Chardonnay (top) and Pinot Noir (bottom), two grape varieties that proved to be well-suited to Santa Barbara County.

Chapter Four

EXPANSION AND EXPERIMENTATION

In the 1980s, one of the best places to be involved in the U.S. wine industry was in Santa Barbara County, where it continued to prosper in the face of nationwide decline. The American wine boom of the 1960s and 1970s had reached a plateau, giving way to a new and difficult economic environment for the industry. Total U.S. wine consumption, which had been rising a phenomenal 11 percent a year on average from 1975 to 1980, slowed sharply in the 1980s and then actually declined every year of that decade after the 1986 peak of 587 million gallons. This reflected a discouraging basic trend: per capita wine consumption was actually slipping downward in the United States.[1]

While the generic wine market slowed, serving and drinking good table wines was an expanding part of the lifestyle of people with disposable income—good news for the Santa Barbara wine region. And the state's premium wine producers were located close to their best consumers: California per capita wine consumption had long been above the national average, and remained so through the 1980s. Further, a weak dollar on international currency exchanges steadily cut the demand for imported premium wines and increased American wine exports. As a final boon to the Santa Barbara region's development, inside the national market for premiums there was a marked shift toward Chardonnay grapes among whites, and Pinot Noir, Cabernet Sauvignon, and Zinfandel among reds. As experience was revealing, Santa Barbara County's cool climate made it prime Chardonnay and Pinot Noir country.

∾ SOME OF THE COUNTY'S FINEST VINEYARDS WERE ESTABLISHED IN COOL VALLEYS WEST OF HIGHWAY 101.

The basic market dynamics of the 1980s kept the state's wine industry under severe pressure, but Santa Barbara County was positioned in a favorable niche. Most important for an exceptional new grape-growing region was the shift in the composition of the wine Americans consumed. Due to rising incomes and increasing sophistication, consumers in the 1980s "dramatically . . . moved upscale," reported San Francisco wine consulting firm Gomberg, Fredrikson & Associates. In Jon Fredrikson's ter-minology, American (and foreign) consumers were increasingly moving their choices up from jug wines to premium wines costing $3 to $7, even to super-premiums from $7 to $12 and ultra-premiums above that—"The silver lining in the gloomy wine picture," he wrote. Through the 1980s the demand grew stronger for premium varietal wines produced from grapes grown in California's cooler, coastal regions. Thus a "premium wine wave," surging from 4 percent of the market in 1980 to 22 percent in 1989, carried Santa Barbara County's grape and wine industry upward—in vineyard acreage, in grape prices, in number of wineries, and in commercial wine sales. The wave was not the answer to all problems for everyone in the region's wine industry, but it was a good ride for the industry as a whole.[2]

By the end of the 1980s, over 9,600 acres of the county were in wine grapes, with 23 county wineries turning 30 percent of the region's grapes into premium wines. (The rest were shipped north either as fruit or juice to improve some other region's wines.) Reflecting both quality and consumer demand for certain varietals, the county's grapes in the 1980s ended the decade more highly priced than those of Sonoma County and just below fruit prices in Napa Valley. Growers had replanted and grafted their way out of a mid-decade price slump caused by planting grapes that did not do well either in the marketplace or in the region's climate. By the end of the decade, grapes were the county's fourth-ranked cash crop, behind broccoli, strawberries, and lettuce.[3]

Getting there, however, was no free ride. The expansion of the 1980s was hard earned, incorporating constant innovation in coping with the whims of nature, guessing which varietals would find consumer favor or flourish on a given hillside, and estimating future demand. Even if growers planted what the market demanded three to five years hence, did they

❧ An increased interest in high-quality wines during the 1980s proved beneficial to Santa Barbara County vineyards and wineries.

choose the right grapes for the site? And then there was "the Government"—federal, state, and local—ever-changing in their tax, labor, and land-use policies.

LEARNING FROM EXPERIENCE: GROWING THE GRAPE

The region had lost whatever lessons had been learned during its first wine experience stretching from mission days to Prohibition. What had been learned in the 1960s and 1970s? When the grape oversupply of the mid-1970s eased a bit, boosters at Bank of America were heard from again, issuing a 1978 report predicting that wine demand in California and the nation would grow six percent a year until at least 1985. State agricultural leaders warned growers not to overplant, advice that was ignored. A new glut of grapes developed in the early 1980s, making "1980, 1981, 1982 . . . tough years," as Rancho Sisquoc's Harold Pfeiffer recalled. The allure of wine was important in motivating entrepreneurs, but it was also a problem. Many people with some capital and little experience "got into the romance of wine," Dale Hampton said, which "created a lot of acres of grapes," and often not the right ones for the site or the market.[4]

Even Hampton admitted to errors in the early plantings. In the Santa Maria Valley "we planted way too damn much Cabernet," he concluded,

WINEMAKER STEPHAN BEDFORD INSPECTS VINES AT THE SANTA MARIA HILLS VINEYARD.

"like it was going out of style," but some sites proved too cold for it. "Pinot [Noir] and Chardonnay, that's it; we shouldn't be in anything else because we are at our best at those two varieties," Hampton concluded, adding that Merlot, Riesling, and Gewurztraminer do well to the south in the interior of the Santa Ynez Valley.

Others in the industry garnered additional lessons. As viticulturist Jeff Newton put it in 1991: "The best Chardonnays and Pinots come from the cooler areas west of U.S. 101 closer to the sea, and the best Sauvignon Blanc and reds like Cabernet from the warmer region to the east. But no one knew this 20 years ago."[5] Stephan Bedford recalls, "We were doing a very

poor job of grape growing in the 1960s and 1970s," among other things attempting to force high yields of six tons an acre to recapture investments when "our cool weather allows only about three."[6]

The solution was to learn how to best grow the grapes the Santa Barbara climate permitted, and to match the varietals demanded by a changing market with the region's microclimates. Initial plantings of Cabernet Sauvignon and sweeter whites such as Riesling, Chenin Blanc, and Gewurztraminer had been excessive, so growers converted to other varietals by replanting and grafting. The shift was heavily toward Chardonnay, which moved up from a mere 227 acres in 1972 to 2,081 acres in 1982 and then 5,381 acres by 1992—59 percent of all grapes in the county.[7]

IMPROVED FARMING TECHNIQUES

Just one percent of Americans grow the food for the other 99, who do not realize that the "traditional" farming sector of the economy is a competitive, fast-changing business in which innovation is a constant factor. Nowhere is this more true than in wine grape farming. In the 1980s, farming practices in Santa Barbara County's expanding vineyards were described by those involved as constant learning from experimentation. Grafting techniques, for example, are as old as the vine itself, but "there are several different ways of grafting," Hampton noted. "A fellow out of Washington . . . created this new grafting technique and . . . we've really done well with that." Row spacing for grapes was a traditional 8 by 12 feet (8 feet between the plants, 12 feet between the rows), but pressures to increase quality and yields led growers to shrink the gaps as low as 6 by 10 feet, the tradeoff being the problem this posed for tractors, especially on hillsides. From Australia came the idea to "hedge the vine like a bush" for easier picking, and the use of an Australian mechanical harvester to pick half the grapes with the other half picked by hand. Drip systems became universal because of their water efficiency and ability to reduce mildew, with sprinklers used only for

↜ Winemaker Bruce McGuire and owner Pierre Lafond try barrel samples at Santa Barbara Winery.

frost control. Vines in the region need far less water than other crops (about half an acre foot per year as opposed to 3.5 acre feet needed for strawberries), and experience revealed that light watering could help bring up the sugar level in the fruit.

To grow crops for people is also to fight off rival consumers—pests. Broccoli and strawberry farmers in the region deployed pesticides to control insects, but wine grape growers were in a different market. Their product wound up in the care of winemakers, who often objected to pesticides: "The more chemicals you put on in the vineyard," said Jim Clendenen, one of the decade's talented new winemakers, "the more problems we have in the winery."[8] One path to reduced pesticide use was the environmentalists' favorite—integrated pest management—and many regional vineyards adopted versions of it. Thus pesticide use in the vineyards tended to be relatively low. Low water use, low pesticides—this made grape growers good agricultural neighbors.

Problems were the drivers of innovation, and innovation was shared and spread throughout the wine industry at a rapid rate—a statewide pattern that also developed in Santa Barbara County. The business was intensely competitive from top to bottom, but from the outset the region's growers and winemakers developed a communal, sharing style. "That's one thing about Santa Barbara

[and] San Luis Obispo counties," Hampton pointed out. "One of the best things you can find. You can ask anybody anything and they'd tell you. There's no holding back. . . . We're not competing against each other, really; we're actually going out there together." This sharing of information among competitors would remain a distinctive feature of the wine culture, and it was especially pronounced in Santa Barbara County.[9]

From Grapes to Wine: The Widening Circle of Winemakers

A grower will tell you that "wines are made in the vineyard,"[10] but wineries turn grapes into wine, which they market in pleasant tasting rooms or on the shelves of stores. The importance of the vineyard is no greater, a diplomat would say, than the role of those who turn grapes into wine.

As the 1980s began, there were 13 bonded wineries in the county; when the decade ended there were 29.[11] Some wineries were large—Firestone turned out 100,000 cases a year—and some were small, producing no more than several thousand cases annually. And in other ways the winemakers of Santa Barbara County presented vastly different wines and settings for winetasting and conversation. Since there had always been many niches in the wine market, the variety was not a sign of confusion, but rather a sign of pursuing many paths to the various tastes of a wine-appreciating public.

WINERIES IN SANTA BARBARA COUNTY: THE 1980S

*T*he 1980s saw a tremendous increase in the number of Santa Barbara County vineyards, wineries, winemakers, and tasting rooms. A growing number of visitors came to the North County's grape-growing region, seeking out wineries that had chosen a tourist orientation. These enterprises usually encompassed a tasting room near a convenient parking lot, surrounded by vines either bare or loaded with fruit, depending on the season. Leading the way, Firestone's brown-timbered winery on a ridge north of Los Olivos was the first and largest of these to be built. The vineyard was established in 1972 and the winery built a few years later,

❧ WINTER AT THE GAINEY VINEYARD (SNOW-CAPPED SAN RAFAEL MOUNTAINS IN THE BACKGROUND).

❧ ALISON GREEN DORAN BECAME WINEMAKER AT FIRESTONE VINEYARD IN 1981.

its cool caverns of tanks and oak barrels extensive enough to accommodate two tours simultaneously.

Santa Barbara Winery, the oldest in the county, had early on decided to locate its tasting room out of the vineyards entirely—in downtown Santa Barbara. Winemaker Bruce McGuire came on board in 1981, and still does his winemaking in the back of the building that houses the tasting room on Anacapa Street, two blocks from the beach. The winery also went beyond the tourist trade, encouraging locals to hold fundraising dinners and other events at the site.

In 1981, two additional wineries opened in-town tasting rooms: Stearns Wharf Vintners began serving their wines at their namesake

location—on Stearns Wharf at the harbor—while Anthony Austin established his tasting room in the town of Los Olivos. Alison Green Doran succeeded Austin as Firestone's winemaker. Located miles away from his 10-acre vineyard, Austin's tasting room sold wines under the Austin Cellars label until 1992.[12]

Taking the visitor trade a step higher was The Gainey Vineyard, with its large, Spanish-styled facility on a vine-clad slope within sight of Highway 246 just north of the Santa Ynez River. Dan Gainey added grapes to his wheat, sugar beet, and cattle ranch in 1984, building the visitor-oriented winery even as the vines went in the ground and then scheduling a series of outdoor summer concerts,

☙ TOP: ELI PARKER, WINEMAKER, FESS PARKER WINERY.
BOTTOM: RACKING BARRELS AT CAMBRIA WINERY.

festive dinners, and a Harvest Day Crush. On Alamo Pintado Road, which runs from Solvang north to Los Olivos, Carey Cellars (now Foley Estates) attracted visitors who would eat lunch or just relax under the shade of a gazebo at the front of the house while viewing the vineyards below.

Toward the end of the decade, two more large-scale wineries made their entrance. One was the 714-acre Fess Parker Winery and Vineyard, located a few miles up Foxen Canyon Road on a high mesa north of Los Olivos. Parker, the man in Davy Crockett's coonskin cap in an earlier career, confesses that his cultural background did not incline him toward wine, but his wife served good wines in their Los Angeles home and he had traveled the Foxen Canyon Road for 25 years with "Firestone and Zaca Mesa to look at." Increasingly drawn to this use of the land, Parker visited Napa Valley in the 1970s, consulted experts at the UC Davis Department of Viticulture and Enology, and talked with friends Brooks Firestone and Dale Hampton. In 1987 he bought the ranch on Foxen Canyon Road and decided he had learned enough to take the plunge into grape growing.

Parker viewed his own inexperience as something of an advantage, figuring that "if you know too much about something you are not likely to do it."[13] The family built a winery with an impressive visitor's facility that included a 35-foot cathedral ceiling, massive fireplace, picnic grounds, and tasting room large enough for special events attracting up to 650 people. The manager, Parker's son Eli, learned winemaking under Jed Steele and hoped to produce 30,000 to 40,000 cases annually. Fess Parker's reputation as an actor no doubt increased the flow of wine tourists up the winding canyon road. The quality of wines was soon notable as well, enough so

that President Bush included Parker's wines at the opening of the Ronald Reagan Presidential Library.

The highest production winery in the county also saw its beginnings in 1987, when a limited partnership—which included Robert Mondavi and San Francisco attorney Jess Jackson—purchased the economically ailing Tepusquet Vineyard. Hoping to take advantage of the highly prized Chardonnay and Pinot Noir grapes being produced in the region, Jackson and his wife, Barbara Banke, established Cambria Winery and Vineyard on the Santa Maria bench property in 1988, which soon had the region's highest volume: By the mid-1990s the winery was producing 150,000 cases

☙ AT BECKMEN VINEYARDS (FORMERLY HOUTZ) THE WINERY IS SURROUNDED BY VINEYARDS AND INVITING PICNIC AREAS.

of "mega-boutique" wines per year
from local grapes and warehousing
over 350,000 cases of Kendall-Jackson
wines from other locations. According
to Jackson, he had seen a "hole in the
market he could drive a truck
through," and thus established
Cambria Winery on the formula of
"quality wine at a bargain price."
While the plan for the 84,000-square-
foot facility included amenities for a
high volume of visitor traffic, it
encountered difficulties in the permit
process that left the winery without a
tasting room and with only limited
access for visitors. Still, Jackson refers
to Cambria as the "jewel of the
Kendall-Jackson chain of small wineries,"[14] an empire that comprises more
than 5,000 acres in Mendocino, Lake,
Sonoma, Napa, Monterey, and Santa
Barbara counties.

Large-scale or highly visible
wineries could take advantage of a
continuous stream of tourist traffic or
high-volume sales through a sizeable
parent corporation, but smaller
wineries or those off the beaten path
had to rely on other means to attract
visitors. Many of these wineries decided to do their marketing and public
relations directly to visitors in settings
offering wine tasting and education,
surrounded by the ambiance of farm
sheds and equipment and orderly
rows of vines, green most of the year.
Wine tourists attracted to Santa
Maria's Tepusquet Mesa, could, after
1984, visit the wooden two-story

LIGHT SHINES FROM THE WINERY AT BUTTONWOOD FARM AT SUNSET.

Byron Winery and tasting room built
along Tepusquet Creek. It was here,
north of the Santa Maria River, that
Ken Brown acquired the original
DeMattei-Nielson and Fesler vineyards and established Byron Winery.
(Later, Brown would sell to Robert
Mondavi, but remain at the facility as
winemaker and general manager.)

Only travellers specifically looking
for the unpretentious sign would find
an arrow directing them up the gravel
road to the 50-acre Babcock Vineyards,
which established its small, rustic winery and tasting room in 1984. The following year, David and Margy Houtz
decided that their Houtz Winery (now

Beckmen), established near Ballard,
would draw exclusively from their
16-acre vineyard that shared space on
a 38-acre farm growing apples and
almonds and raising chickens and
guinea hens. One permanent employee
seemed enough to handle the expected visitor flow.

In the Santa Ynez Valley, Betty
Williams and Bret Davenport had
started grapes on their thoroughbred
ranch in 1983, thus launching
Buttonwood Farm Winery on a west-
facing slope along Alamo Pintado
Road between Santa Ynez and Los
Olivos. They employed a motley,
enthusiastic crew of students from

UC Santa Barbara. ("You could tell they weren't planning to spend all their lives working in the fields," recalled Williams).[15] Their winery was built in 1988, with wine tasting inside and produce stalls selling farm vegetables outside. Another new winery with rural appeal was Foxen Vineyard, established in 1987. When the tasting room was open and the sign was out, visitors driving down Foxen Canyon Road toward the Santa Maria River couldn't miss Foxen's converted farm buildings. Located just off the narrow road, the rustic structures beckoned them to an intimate tasting room, where they could sample from Foxen's planned output of 1,000 cases per year—a figure that has since risen to over 5,000 cases.

☙ Above: Much of the grape crop is harvested by hand.
Right: Industry or agriculture? Zoning and tax laws were debated by county government in the late 1970s, eventually favoring the construction of more wineries.

Wineries in Warehouses

Although many new wineries opened a tasting or visitor facility close to the winemaking and vineyards and included an on-site marketing/public relations component, another pattern was emerging for those determined to make wines under their own label but unable to afford vineyard acreage. Winemakers could work in space rented anywhere, even a barn or an urban warehouse. As a financial and managerial consideration, there were costs in building, staffing, and managing a tasting room and tours, an important issue for individuals with little capital who preferred to concentrate upon the wine and believed that marketing could be

done in other ways. Why spend scarce money and time managing visitors, when you could devote your time to winemaking and the necessary travel to restaurants, buyers, and special events for marketing? This was apparently the reasoning of several new entrants into the wine business in the 1980s.

For a time it seemed that local government might disallow this option. Wineries of any kind were a novelty in the 1970s, and a pro-agricultural county government wondered if wineries were "industry" and thus suspect. A first grapple with this concern came when the Firestone and Santa Ynez wineries asked for conditional use permits for facilities. County officials voiced concerns about increased traffic and roadside commerce they felt could take on a tone unbefitting to Santa Barbara County. "Unless restrictions were laid down, a number of them might be strung along principal highways as roadside wine stands," a planning commissioner declared. It was finally decided, however, that "a winery is an agricultural use," and the permits went through.[16]

But if a winery was agriculture (even though it looked like manufacturing), should it get the favorable treatment farmers did? Should the acre of ground on which a winery stood therefore qualify for Williamson Act tax benefits just as the acre of grapes next to it? In 1977 County

Farm Advisor George Goodall apparently convinced the Board of Supervisors that grapes were a "unique crop"—agriculture all the way to the bottle![17] The subsidy was granted, and the battle to accept wineries in an agricultural region was being won.

Yet wineries functioning in warehouses, a development of the 1980s, bothered authorities. Physically disconnected from agriculture, might they become merely large wine factories—a form of industrial sprawl?

In 1982 the county Planning Commission proposed a requirement that all local winemakers must also become farmers, growing at least half the grapes they use. With winemaking and grape farming such different undertakings, neither growers nor winemakers felt this was a possibility, which they explained to the county supervisors. The regulation was then modified to require half a winery's grapes to come "from the wine growing area" of Santa Barbara and San Luis Obispo counties, preserving the winemakers' flexibility in choosing grapes and deciding where to turn them into wine.[18]

This route was initially taken by Richard Sanford when a difference of opinion over winemaking led to the dissolution of his partnership with Michael Benedict in 1980. Benedict kept the vineyard, while Sanford, his wife Thekla, and winemaker Bruno D'Alfonso moved the winery equipment to a Buellton warehouse and began bottling under the Sanford Winery label in 1983. Sanford later recalled how, a year later, "I couldn't even sell my 6,000 cases of Pinot Noir." Denied access to Sanford and Benedict fruit, the vintners at Sanford Winery had to "relearn" winemaking with grapes from less familiar vineyards in the area. After his former partner sold the vineyard to British financier Robert Atkin, however, Sanford regained control of the vines he had helped plant more than a decade earlier. Convinced of the impact proper management had on the value of vineyards, Atkin hired Sanford as a full-time vineyard manager and promised the Sanford Winery a steady supply of premium-quality grapes. The winery eventually expanded to include a rustic tasting room at the end of a gravel road that runs, as visitors expect, through a few acres of vines sloping up from the Santa Ynez River.[19]

Many winemakers never intended to open their doors to the public, however. Some made wine for established wineries while maintaining their own label on the side. Rick Longoria became the Gainey Vineyard winemaker after short stints at J. Carey and Rancho Sisquoc. While at Gainey he established his Longoria label with the help of his wife, Diana, and startup capital from his father. Mike Brown worked alternating crushes in Australia and Santa

⌘ MIKE BROWN, WINEMAKER FOR BUTTONWOOD FARM WINERY, ALSO PRODUCES WINE UNDER HIS OWN KALYRA LABEL.

Barbara between 1982 and 1987 and became winemaker for Buttonwood Farm Winery in 1989. Like Longoria, he also used his stable winemaker position as an opportunity to produce his own wines under the Kalyra label.

UC Santa Barbara graduate Jim Clendenen had intended to be a lawyer, but in 1978 he became the second employee hired at Zaca Mesa Winery, working under Ken Brown to run the bottling line. For Jim, Zaca Mesa was like a three-year graduate course in winemaking, which he followed with a postgraduate tour in Australia and France in 1981, building intellectual capital despite lacking the

❧ ABOVE: SINCE 1984, JOHN KERR, WINEMAKER FOR FOLEY ESTATES, HAS MADE WINE AT BABCOCK, BRANDER, HOUTZ, BYRON, AND CAREY CELLARS, AND PRODUCED HIS OWN LABEL FROM 1986-'96. RIGHT: LANE TANNER SPECIALIZES IN PINOT NOIRS.

financial kind. Clendenen met Adam Tolmach at Zaca Mesa in 1979, and the two started Au Bon Climat Winery in 1982, operating in an abandoned dairy farm in Los Alamos. Clendenen assumed ownership in 1991, and at the invitation of Bob and Steve Miller, moved his winemaking to a site at Bien Nacido Vineyards east of Santa Maria. Proving that good wine could find buyers without on-site tasting, Au Bon Climat grew from producing 1,600 to 10,000 cases in a decade.[20]

Qupé (the Chumash term for "poppy") was founded in 1982 by another "graduate" of Zaca Mesa, Bob Lindquist. (The three schools for winemakers, judging from local experience, are University of California at Davis, California State University at Fresno, and Zaca Mesa Winery.)[21] Like many others, Lindquist borrowed and rented space, first at Zaca Mesa, then at Sanford, and finally at the cooperative winery at Los Vineros. After 1989 Qupé joined Clendenen's Au Bon Climat in a non-tourist winery on Bien Nacido property. Clendenen and Lindquist were bottling competitive and successful labels side by side, later joined by Jim Adelman, Gary Burk, and Frank Ostini, who bottled small batches of their own. Their marketing was done by restaurant visits, newsletters, word of mouth, and through a multi-label wine-tasting room in Los Olivos stocked with wines from other winemakers who lacked on-site visitor facilities. Similar arrangements with two or more winemakers under one roof would become a widespread practice.

Many more winemakers would follow the path taken by Clendenen and Lindquist, producing their wines in rented space that they sometimes shared. Chris Whitcraft launched his label in 1985, making an impression at once with his Whitcraft Chardonnay and producing around 1,000 cases. John Kerr produced his first J. Kerr wines in 1986, working under Ken Brown's roof after hours as assistant winemaker for Byron. Gary Mosby became one of the first second-generation winemakers in Santa Barbara County when he began producing and marketing his own Chimère label wines in 1989. Similar starts occurred as Lane Tanner, an early Zaca Mesa employee and winemaker for the Hitching Post Restaurant label, established a "one-woman winemaking operation" bearing her name in 1989.[22]

THE SHAPE OF THE REGIONAL INDUSTRY

From the point of view of the consumer, the region's wine industry by the 1980s was developing an admirable diversity. For wine tourists, eager for a rural vacation away from the crowded urban scene in Southern California or elsewhere, the county offered a garland of wineries large and small, arranged in a rough triangle stretching across the Santa Maria, Los Alamos, and Santa Ynez valleys. These were open to the public during scheduled hours, offering tasting and tours—a chance to see the product in the making, whether in the hectic activity of crush or the sequestered aging of barrels or tanks. For suburbanites from the Los Angeles area, wine touring required only a two-hour drive up the coast. There, Santa Barbara County spread out north of the Santa Ynez Mountains, a rural setting in which to bike or drive to where wine was made. Surrounded by views of the oak-studded, rolling hills, visitors could experience the coastal California that existed before the onset of widespread urbanization. And for wine aficionados with no immediate plans to visit the area—people living in San Francisco, Washington, New York, London, or Tokyo—Santa Barbara County had, in a short 20 years, enlarged the choice of labels associated with wines of excellence and distinctiveness.

The county's wine industry very much embraced a western sense of social fluidity: Some people came to the industry through longstanding family traditions, but others could still start from scratch. Sanford and Benedict began with no formal training in either growing or winemaking, while Tony Austin was a fourth-generation native of Sonoma County wine country who studied viticulture at UC Davis under the master, André Tchelistcheff. Fess Parker did not even like wine for many years. Brooks

Firestone came from eastern industry, but Richard Doré of Foxen Vineyard grew up on ranch land in the Santa Maria Valley that had been in the family since 1847. He formed a partnership with Bill Wathen, a Cal Poly viticulture graduate who had been involved in some of Santa Barbara County's early vineyards and had worked at Chalone in Monterey County. Lane Tanner started labeling bottles at a Sonoma winery where she met Tchelistcheff, who sent her to work at Firestone and then to Zaca Mesa. John Kerr apprenticed in tasting rooms in Ventura County, and at Chalone, Babcock,

∾ TOP: SPRINGTIME AT ANDREW MURRAY VINEYARDS SHOWING THE LOVELY RURAL SCENERY THAT ATTRACTS MANY WINE TOURISTS TO SANTA BARBARA COUNTY.
BOTTOM: DICK DORÉ AND BILL WATHEN IN THE TASTING ROOM AT FOXEN VINEYARD.

Houtz, and Brander wineries, but Chris Whitcraft trained as a manager of a wine store in Montecito. The industry was remarkably open to new talent, including women such as winery owners Kate Firestone, Margy Houtz, and Barbara Banke and winemakers Lane Tanner, Kathy Joseph, and Alison Green Doran. It was an open rather than a closed world.

THE MOST UNECONOMIC ITEM

A small winery, as anyone knows who has been in the business, is the most uneconomic item that you could possibly get involved in," reflected Kate Firestone after she was immersed in the business of Carey Cellars.[23] Although the region's wine industry was largely successful

∾ "PUNCHING DOWN" HELPS BREAK UP AND SUBMERGE THE CAP OF SKINS AND OTHER SOLIDS DURING RED WINE FERMENTATION.

after the 1960s, the economic reality under the eye-catching growth was that making it in any part of the wine business was hard—harder than anybody thought when "we all started dreaming about it." What did a dentist or an oil executive know, starting out, about growing grapes? What did a table grape grower from the Central Valley know about growing premium wine grapes? What did a botanist or geographer know about turning grapes into wine? If anybody could find Ben Alfonso, one of the few people in the county who made wine commercially after Prohibition, would he know where to plant certain varietals? What did *anybody* new to this business know about wine marketing in the changing national and international wine markets after the 1960s?

"If you want to make a small fortune in the wine business, then start with a large one," the saying goes. This sums up a lot that was learned across California in the decades after the 1960s. The wine business, with all of its romantic associations, is a part of American capitalism, and therefore a tough school in which the survivors are fast learners and adapters. Planting the wrong grapes in a promising place is an expensive error, but only by trial and error did growers learn about the subtle influence of microclimates on wine grapes. If by luck or quick corrections you get your vineyard producing excellent fruit and a talented winemaker makes no mistakes, marketing to

wine stores, supermarkets, and restaurants is a fierce struggle requiring additional time and skill. Then the federal and state governments impose costs: "We basically have had to hire one to one-and-a-half people to deal with the federal and state regulations and the paperwork that is required," said Hayley Firestone Jessup, retail operations manager at Firestone Vineyard. ("Overwhelming," was Kate Firestone's rough calculation.)[24]

There were losses along the way. In addition to Tepusquet Vineyard's financial difficulties and sale to Mondavi and Jackson, other vineyards that were forced into bankruptcy or selling out included Los Alamos, Greenleaf Farm, Sierra Madre, Cat Canyon, and White Hills. This was a statewide phenomenon, and in Santa Barbara County as elsewhere, vineyards unable to carry their loans went initially into the hands of lenders like Prudential Life Insurance Company or Wells Fargo Bank, who sold the properties as soon as it became convenient. The new buyers were not graduate students or retired professionals, but more often large-volume wineries from the north.[25] All in all, in the late 1980s Northern California wineries bought $36 million worth of vineyards in Santa Barbara and San Luis Obispo counties—the ultimate compliment to the south central coast's performance and promise.[26]

The first generation of wineries, too, experienced growing pains. Some wineries closed—such as Ballard Canyon—and others endured financial difficulties that lead to reorganization, which was the case with Zaca Mesa. In 1980 the Davidges and Bettencourts had joined up with vineyard owners George Ott, Eric Caldwell, Charlotte Young, Uriel Nielson, and Bob Woods to form Los Vineros, a cooperative winery that would take their grapes. They had mastered the growing and winemaking phases far better than the marketing, however, and closed in 1986.[27] The public record only hints at the losses of early investors such as these, but the visible part of the story shows stubborn, tenacious survivors, building reputations and slowly expanding their sales. Grape acreage in the county stabilized in the late 1980s at about 10,000 acres, and the number of wineries climbed toward 30.[28]

One result of the intense competitive pressures within the growing local wine industry was the major infusion of capital in the 1980s, when large, prestigious wineries of the Napa-Sonoma region began buying Santa Barbara vineyards. By the early 1990s, 39 percent of the county's grapes were shipped north to out-of-county wineries from Santa Barbara acreage they owned, with another 26 percent sold under contract to other winemakers ouside the county. That left 35 percent of the county's grapes to be made into local-label wine, creating two potential problems.[29] "The fact that most of the

grapes are vinified elsewhere has created real identity problems for the south central coast," Ken Brown told *Wine Spectator.*[30] "Napa owns us," complained another grower. "They use us to pick up their quality."[31] Was the emerging regional identity for high quality grapes being siphoned off into other region's products, leaving a shrinking base of vineyards under local winery control?

If the maintenance of regional identity seemed potentially threatened by "foreign capital" entering into the county's vineyard markets, the sheer availability of quality grapes concerned individual area winemakers

↬ Top: Mission Trails vineyard is owned by Kendall-Jackson, one of several northern California wineries to increase holdings in Santa Barbara County during the 1980s. Bottom: Byron "Ken" Brown remained winemaker for Byron Vineyard and Winery after it was purchased by Robert Mondavi.

with little or no land in vines.[32] "I thought I was out of business," recalled Richard Sanford, whose wine volume outstripped the capacity of his own vineyard. Jim Clendenen felt the same pressure:

In 1988, I almost went out of business. It was real hard to buy grapes at all.... If we didn't find growers that would cooperate with us every year and weren't interested in selling their vineyards....[and] having a good relationship with a winery year in and year out...then we'd be, every year, open to the vagaries of having our production source sold and sooner or later, we'd have been out of business for sure.

◆ Jeff Newton manages many Santa Ynez Valley vineyards.

They did not go out of business, though. Something quite different happened, at least in the short run. There is some evidence that a more stable local supplier-local winery

relationship was indeed developing as the industry matured. Some regional growers recognized the importance of local wineries and their region-promoting labels and products. When Dale Hampton, TV producer Douglas S. Cramer, and Zaca Mesa owner John C. Cushman formed a partnership to buy Sierra Madre Vineyard in 1988, Hampton felt the purchase would enable them "to keep these grapes in the county and ensure the continuing quality and reputation of the grapes."[33] Concerns for preserving the reputation of the county's premium wine grapes were well founded: By 1995 over 6,000 of the region's total 10,000 acres would belong to Wine World, Kendall-Jackson, and Mondavi, due to aggressive land and vineyard purchases.[34]

Longer-term grape contracts and closer ties with growers allowed winemakers to influence the growers toward higher grape quality at the expense of sheer tonnage. Grape farmers occasionally saw it differently. To some local growers, the Napa-Sonoma vineyard purchases were good for the Santa Barbara industry in ways not foreseen. If anybody had doubted it, the eagerness of Napa-Sonoma firms to buy Santa Barbara County fruit "lends credence to the fact that some good quality fruit is here," said Bill Spencer, former winemaker for Santa Ynez Winery.[35] Jeff Newton predicted that large northern wineries would make much use of the

Santa Barbara name, and thereby generate a beneficial "coattail" effect for local wineries.[36] And while the surge of vineyard buying drove grape prices up and squeezed local winemakers, Santa Barbara growers saw much good in that too. Purchases of Central Coast vineyards by Bay Area companies pushed prices up. With higher prices and rising land values in the vineyards, "you saw a lot more seriousness in the vineyard," winemaker Stephan Bedford recalled, also attributing some of the improved growing techniques to the skills that came in with northern capital. "I think ultimately what you saw," he concluded, "was higher wine quality." Tough times in the 1980s had consolidated the industry to some degree by wringing out some of the early vineyard entrepreneurs and stabilizing local winery-grower relationships, both with the same result: wine of rising quality.[37]

RECOGNITION AND REPUTATION

*T*he high quality of local grapes and wines rapidly put Santa Barbara County on the international wine map, which for so long had been dominated by Bay Area wine regions. Following the scattered awards and reviews in the late 1970s, a volley of prizes to area wines punctuated every year in the 1980s and on into the '90s, such as the International Wine Center's recognition of Zaca Mesa's

1983 Central Coast Cabernet as one of the best red wines priced under $10. Ronald Reagan, whose ranch sat high in the Santa Ynez mountains between Santa Barbara and the northern valleys, invited Brooks Firestone to his inauguration and served Santa Barbara County wines on many occasions, with one Brander Sauvignon Blanc receiving compliments from French President Francois Mitterand at a state function. When Bill Clinton entered the White House, Richard Sanford's labels appeared at official functions.[38] Another sign of increasing regional visibility came in wine guidebooks.[39] By the 1990s the county's vineyards, wineries, and wines were described in dozens of wine encyclopedias and guidebooks.

Thus the area's recognition went beyond visibility as a tourist destination for tasters, translating into penetration into markets farther away than even the White House dining rooms. In the early '90s, one of the authors stopped in a health food market in Chapel Hill, North Carolina, cornerstone of the high-tech and university-dense "Triangle" metropolis, and found Lane Tanner's Pinot Noir on the shelf. Bob Lindquist's Qupé winery found it was selling 55 percent of its annual production in California, the rest in 24 other states and in Canada, England, Switzerland, Germany, and Japan. Santa Barbara's new, fledgling wine industry, just 25 years old, had arrived. ❧

AMERICAN VITICULTURAL AREAS OF SANTA BARBARA COUNTY

When a region's wines in France achieve public approval as distinctive and desirable, the French confer an appellation, which guarantees the consumer that the wine in the bottle really came from the grapes and winemakers of that locale. Strict controls go with European appellations. The American equivalent, with fewer controls, was launched by Congress in 1978 when it established a system of American Viticultural Areas (AVAs) to be conferred by Bureau of Alcohol, Tobacco, and Firearms (BATF) upon application by an area's winemakers. Petitioning BATF for an AVA designation makes sense when consumers have decided that an area's wines have a distinctive taste and are of high quality. Wine writer Matt Kramer refers to it as the "somewhereness" of wine.

Santa Barbara County was awarded its first appellation for a winemaking area in 1981 when Santa Maria Valley vintners received the right to put an AVA designation on their labels. The Santa Ynez Valley became an AVA in 1983. They had built a fence around a distinctive wine quality, and, with federal approval, announced it to the world. The designation did not so much create regional recognition as reflect it. (See maps on pages 62-63 for AVAs in Santa Barbara County.)[40]

❧ TOP: THE SANTA YNEZ VALLEY APPELLATION INCLUDES VINEYARDS ON BOTH SIDES OF THE SANTA YNEZ RIVER.
BOTTOM: THOUSANDS OF ACRES ARE PLANTED IN THE SANTA MARIA VALLEY APPELLATION EAST OF HIGHWAY 101.

Chapter Five

RECOGNITION AND IDENTITY

One measure of the Santa Barbara County wine industry's impact is the size it has achieved in a single generation. By 1996, in a county in which agriculture was still the leading source of income, grapes were the third crop in market value. The value added by turning grapes into wine—an additional $69 million—puts the industry well into first place. If tourist revenues from wine tourism (estimated at 200,000 visits annually) are shifted to the wine industry column, its economic impact on the region looms even larger.[1]

These figures represent economic activity that had not been taking place in the region 30 years earlier—jobs, profits, spillover effects to suppliers. A new export industry reaching distant markets had been planted—actually replanted—in Santa Barbara County soil. In 1989, vineyards were selling 70 percent of the grape crop to northern buyers, whose eagerness for the product drove Santa Barbara grape prices to a rank comparable to Napa's, the fastest rate of price increase for any California region. By 1996, however, only 56 percent of Santa Barbara's wine grapes were being shipped outside the county, and the majority of these went to wineries that were affiliated with local vineyards. Moreover, the local vintners produced more than 780,000 cases of wine that year, most of them in the super-premium category, averaging $12 to $14 a bottle at retail.[2] About 15 percent of that wine was consumed in Santa Barbara County, 24 percent was purchased by other Californians, and the remaining

~ TINAQUAIC VINEYARD PROVIDES THE GRAPES FOR THE ESTATE WINES MADE BY FOXEN VINEYARD .

61 percent was shipped to other states or abroad. During the 1990s California wine exports as a whole increased nearly sevenfold as the state's wineries poured their efforts into building an international reputation.[3] Santa Barbara County's climate, soils, and human skills were appreciated in both near and distant places.

~ Kathy Joseph, owner-vintner of Fiddlehead Cellars, checks just-harvested Sauvignon Blanc grapes.

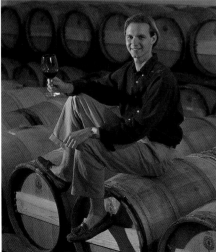

~ Top: The winery at Andrew Murray Vineyards.
Bottom: Andrew Murray in the barrel room.

The revived Santa Barbara wine industry continues to add new entrants. Andrew Murray Vineyards (Jim and Fran Murray named the place after their son and winemaker, Andrew) planted their first grapes in 1991 and built their winery just up Foxen Canyon Road from Fess Parker. Owner-vintner Kathy Joseph of Fiddlehead Cellars moved to the Santa Barbara area from Napa. Fred and Linda Rice opened Sunstone Winery's facility with a tasting room facing south toward the Santa Ynez River just a short distance from Solvang. Sunstone's winemaker Doug Braun also produced wine under his Presidio Wines label. Gerry Moro (Morovino), Craig Jaffurs (Jaffurs Wine Cellars), and Ardison Phillips (McKeon-Phillips Wines) joined John Kerr, Lane Tanner, and Chris Whitcraft in the expanding Central Coast Wine Warehouse. Zaca Mesa's new majority owner, John Cushman, brought in a new general manager, Jeff Maiken, and a new winemaker, Daniel Gehrs; a new marketing plan and a range of production changes turned sales upward for the winery that had trained so many vintners and seen them set up competing labels. Tony Austin sold his Austin Cellars to the Santa Ynez Wine Corporation, which renamed the winery Los Olivos Vintners, and Ballard Canyon Winery was revitalized by Geoff and Alison Rusack, who renamed it Rusack Vineyards.

But while new wineries continue to appear, one thing has changed, at least in Jim Clendenen's view. Could he start Au Bon Climat in the 1990s, as he had done 20 years before, on $50,000 of borrowed capital? "I say no and I believe no," he concluded in 1994. All the prices are higher: grapes, glass, barrels. Newcomers will still enter the industry, but Clendenen spoke somewhat wistfully of a time when the bar had been a bit lower for the next generation.[4]

A Unique Part of Regional Agriculture

The wine industry that developed in Santa Barbara County was in a sense miscast when, in 1996, wine grapes became the third-ranked agricultural product in the county, just behind strawberries and broccoli. "When ranked based upon assets employed," the Gomberg, Fredrikson & Associates report notes, "the wine industry, with approximately $142 million in assets, probably is the largest or nearly the largest agricultural business in the county."[5] Premium winemaking began as agriculture but it ended in manufacturing, a rural but high-tech manufacturing process requiring intensive research, experimentation, and front-end investment years before a return could be realized. Both in the growing of grapes and in winemaking there is a strong aesthetic component, an awareness that the final measure of success will be highly refined consumer judgments about taste, aroma, and price. To be in the local wine industry, with an intense "fine wine ambition" and vision of excellence that is never fully satisfied, requires one to know more than just soil, weather, and marketing. The wine industry, from the vineyard through the bottling rooms to the university enology laboratories, absorbs as well as generates cutting-edge knowledge of botany and chemistry, geography and hydrology. And it is an enterprise that is steeped in history and cultural symbolism. Thus the rank of third in Santa Barbara County agriculture, one could say, went not to a crop but to a unique way of life.

Despite wine's ancient lineage and the impressive centuries of continuity

☙ ABOVE: THE BARREL CAVE AT SUNSTONE WINERY.
RIGHT: DAN GEHRS AND VINEYARD MANAGER RUBEN CAMACHO INSPECT GRAPES AT ZACA MESA.

in its symbolisms and rituals, the industry here has been the opposite of settled and static. Market forces and on-the-ground experimentation in Santa Barbara County's microclimates since the 1960s had radically altered the varietals planted or grafted for harvest. Early enthusiasm for White Riesling, Chenin Blanc, and Cabernet Sauvignon was corrected by experience. Acres of these varietals were shifted to

∾ Top, left to right: Zaca Mesa "Alumni series" winemakers Jim Clendenen, Dan Gehrs, Lane Tanner, and Bob Lindquist. Bottom: Viognier is one of several varietals newly planted in Santa Barbara County in the early 1990s.

the dominant Chardonnay, while a small boom of Merlot sales and appreciation was the talk of the red wine segment.[6] Restless experimenters still branch off from the basic Burgundian varietals that have been the region's mainstay. Bill Mosby at Mosby Winery started early with growing Italian varieties, and now produces (among other novelties) a Brunello wine similar to Chianti; Bob Lindquist of Qupé pursues the elusive qualities of the Rhone varietal Syrah; and Andrew Murray Vineyards in the early 1990s put in 20 acres of Rhone grapes that required new spelling skills—Viognier, Roussanne, Marsanne, and Mourvedre. In 1993, Mosby Winery won a double gold medal award at the San Francisco Fair with another inno-

vation, Grappa de Traminer—a handcrafted spirit distilled in small batches under the county's first distilled spirits permit.[7]

Experimentation also took the form of changing the vineyard's shape, as could be seen in the 1990s on Fred Brander's 42-acre Los Olivos vineyard where "high-density" planting spaced vines 4 feet apart in both directions, radically altering the exposure to sun and, as European experiments had shown, the flavor of the fruit. In the words of Steve Pitcher, former wine columnist for the *San Francisco Chronicle*, Santa Barbara seems to have attracted "an extremely innovative group of winemakers"— and growers, he might have added, sometimes the two being the same. "A small voice can be heard a lot louder here," adds Fred Brander. "Without a track record, the vintners here were more open to try new varieties and blends. Here you'll find more the maverick type, the guy who's not always watching the bottom line."[8]

CAMARADERIE, COLLABORATION, AND A COOPERATIVE SPIRIT

Since the wine business is closely tied to agriculture, there is a seasonal rhythm to it. One thing that visitors will not see at a tasting room is vividly evident during the Santa Barbara County Vintners' Association's festivals celebrating the spring sprouting of leaves and the fall crush of the grapes—the spirit of camaraderie that unifies the county's more than 30 competing wineries. At festival time, winery owners and staff pitch their tents side-by-side, and an observer is likely to spot a vintner under some other winery's canvas sharing stories. But the cooperative spirit goes deeper than the two annual festivals sponsored by the association. Three highly successful winemakers who left Zaca Mesa to launch their own competitive labels—Jim Clendenen, Bob Lindquist, and Lane Tanner—returned in the early '90s at the invitation of Jeff Maiken and Daniel Gehrs to produce an "Alumni Series" of wines made from Zaca Mesa grapes under a Zaca Mesa label with the signature of the guest winemaker. "I don't know of any other area where people who own their own winery will go back to another (winery) just to help it go," Tanner observed.

An even stronger demonstration of the strong sense of cohesiveness among area winemakers came in 1990 when Richard Sanford secured the financing to regain control of the highly regarded Sanford and Benedict Vineyard that he and Michael Benedict had planted in 1972. Sanford announced plans to use all of the grapes from the vineyard, grapes that for years Benedict had been selling to the highest bidders. Local vintners—Sanford's competitors in one sense, in another his regional allies—protested the loss of the grapes, the Pinot Noirs

especially. In response, Sanford and his winemaker, Bruno D'Alfonso, agreed to sell some of his prized Pinot Noir grapes to five other wineries—Foxen, Lane Tanner, Babcock, Gainey, and Au Bon Climat. Each would return a barrel of their wine, and D'Alfonso would make a composite blend. As Steve Pitcher observed: "The wine industry as a whole is pretty open, but in Santa Barbara County it's like an ongoing seminar. There is a constant exchange of information, a real family-type attitude toward making wine."[9]

THE RIPENING OF RECOGNITION

*S*anta Barbara. . ." announced the headline in *The Wine Advocate* in 1993, "California's Most Exciting Viticultural Region for Chardonnay and Pinot Noir." With or without endorsements such as these, however, the quality of the region's grapes was unsentimentally being measured in the marketplace. In 1992 a survey found Santa Barbara County grapes' average price per ton ($1,011) second only to Napa's ($1,218). From such grapes,

❧ SANFORD WINERY WINEMAKER BRUNO D'ALFONSO AND OWNER RICHARD SANFORD HAVE BEEN A WINE-MAKING TEAM SINCE 1983.

By 1990 Santa Barbara County had earned the reputation as a prime Chardonnay and Pinot Noir grape-growing and winemaking area.
Top: Bob Lindquist of Qupé moves Chardonnay grapes to the press.
Bottom: Workers harvest Pinot Noir at the Sanford & Benedict Vineyard.

area vintners made a product that earned its glowing reputation. At the 1992 Orange County Fair Commercial Wine Competition, 45 wines made by 17 members of the Santa Barbara County Vintners' Association won awards. *The Wine Spectator* placed Byron, Gainey, and Santa Barbara Winery Chardonnays as "top-rated" in the state in 1990; Byron, Sanford, and Firestone in 1991.

Some wine writers-tasters were carried entirely to the end of the scale of approval: "I feel that Santa Barbara has probably the greatest grape-growing area anywhere in the United States, particularly when it comes to great Chardonnay and Pinot Noir," concluded Bernard Epicum, owner of Eclipse restaurant in Los Angeles. Steve Pitcher wrote that "Extraordinary Chardonnay comes from Santa Barbara County, and Sanford Winery's Chardonnay is the benchmark for the county." The 1988 Barrel Select Chardonnay was his "choice for the greatest Chardonnay ever produced in California."

As for the reds, a special reputation for the region's Pinot Noirs was also building. "Santa Barbara is producing so many sumptuous Pinot Noirs . . . the world's most fickle red wine grape," that the county "may be America's most promising area for this varietal," wrote top-ranked wine writer Robert Parker in *Food and Wine Magazine* in 1993. No wine encyclopedia or guidebook in the 1990s failed to note the region's arrival as a wine producer. When French President Jacques Chirac visited the White House in 1996, food and beverage director Daniel Shanks served Zaca Mesa's 1993 Syrah, which scored 94 on *The Wine Spectator's* 100-point scale and was named as one of the Top Ten wines of 1995. After the event, Zaca's owner, John Cushman, had to mine his private cellar to cover the three cases ordered by President Clinton.[10]

Evidence gathered randomly is often the best. Invited to dinner one February evening in Washington, D.C. and wanting to take a gift of wine, one of the authors of this book dropped into The Wine Specialist, a wine store at the corner of M Street and New Hampshire Avenue. After selecting a Firestone Gewurztraminer he asked the salesman: "Do people come in here and ask for wine from Santa Barbara County?"

"Of course, all the time," said the salesman. "They know Santa Barbara County. Of course, we know it, too, because the boss's daughter goes to college there."

"Is that why they ask for it?"

"No, no. It's Pinots, you know. Best Pinot Noir in the country is made there."[11]

Santa Barbara County Vintners' Association

*T*he Santa Barbara County Vintners' Association (SBCVA) grew out of a wine tasting held at Mission Santa Inés in Solvang, April 1983—the first of what was to become the annual Vintners' Festival. The following year, with 17 wineries as founding members, the association was incorporated as a nonprofit organization with the purpose of promoting the wine industry of Santa Barbara County.

In 14 years, the SBCVA has grown to include over 50 members—mostly wineries, but also vineyards and vineyard managers/consultants. The organization's activities also have expanded significantly, including out-of-town and out-of-state tastings for media and trade; educational programs for growers, restaurant staffs, and consumers; media seminars and tours; promotions and advertising; and economic studies. An Associate Membership program provides additional activities and information resources for related industries and individual winelovers.

The annual Santa Barbara County Vintners' Festival became so popular that in 1988 it was expanded to a two-day event and in 1996 it was moved to a site that could accommodate larger numbers of people. To further increase the public's enjoyment of the local wine industry, the SBCVA now also sponsors an annual fall harvest tasting—A Celebration of Harvest. In addition to these annual events, the SBCVA produces visitor-oriented wine touring maps, calendars of wine events, annual Vintners' Festival posters, and shirts.

Executive Directors:

1983-85	Deborah Kenley Brown
1985-87	Diana Longoria
1987-	Pam Maines Ostendorf

Presidents:

1984-85	Bob Lindquist, Qupé
1985-86	Julianne Poirier, Santa Barbara Winery
1986-88	Jim Fiolek, Sanford Winery
1988-91	Barry Johnson, The Gainey Vineyard
1991-94	Patrick Will, Firestone Vineyard
1994-95	Laila Rashid, Santa Barbara Winery
1995-97	Jeff Maiken, Zaca Mesa Winery

LEFT: A CELEBRATION OF HARVEST, 1993, AT FIRESTONE MEADOW. ABOVE: ALL MEMBER WINERIES POUR THEIR FINE WINES AT ASSOCIATION-SPONSORED EVENTS.

Chapter Six

HERE TO STAY

Will Santa Barbara County continue to hold a top-ranking position in the worldwide wine industry? After all, towns in the mountain West boomed with mining, then shrank to insignifance when the vein ran out. Lowell, Massachusetts, was for decades the hub of America's textile industry, until the mills fled south. New Orleans was once a bustling cotton exporter, and knives were made in Toledo, Spain, but today these enterprises no longer flourish there. Industries grow up only to recede, and often migrate away from places where they once thrived. Certainly the history of wine is one vast, restless global migration out of the Caucasus Mountain region in southeastern Europe, the cradle of winemaking. (See Appendix 1.)

While California has indeed vaulted to the top rank among the world's winemaking regions, the state's industry faces challenges that Santa Barbara County shares. The global wine market is not growing at the same rate it did from the 1950s through the 1970s, and the strong hold of premium wine among upscale consumers is not being matched by generic wine consumption at the average dinner table. Indeed, average per-capita wine consumption (except for Chardonnay) actually declined somewhat in the early 1990s.

Against this background of sluggish changes in overall demand, *TIME* magazine unsurprisingly reported that despite its "aura of romance," winemaking was, like any other enterprise, "beset with woes." The boom and bust cycle persisted, but in the 1990s both phases of the cycle seemed to have arrived at the same time. Premium wines—Santa Barbara County's specialty—entered a

~ A LONE OAK SENTINAL AT THE SANFORD & BENEDICT VINEYARD.

period of growth, with national and international demand surging and prices rising at a rate of eight percent a year by mid-decade. The entire California premium wine sector enjoyed increased exports, the value of its overseas sales leaping 437 percent from 1985 to 1995.[1] Below the premium level, however, demand was stagnant, and some said that the state's wine industry was "overbuilt," with too many wineries scrambling for shelf space and attention in an intensely competitive domestic market for ordinary table wines. Inexpensive wines from new regions abroad such as Australia and Chile (and older regions, such as Romania) appeared on American supermarket shelves. Rival regions in the United States were springing into view, with vineyards and wineries emerging in the coastal regions of Washington and Oregon, but also in unlikely places like western

CENTRAL COAST WINE WAREHOUSE PROVIDES WINERY AND STORAGE FACILITIES FOR A NUMBER OF SANTA BARBARA COUNTY WINEMAKERS.

STEARNS WHARF VINTNERS' DECK IS A SCENIC SPOT FOR WINE TASTING AT THE BEACH IN SANTA BARBARA.

Colorado, Texas, Virginia, North Carolina, Georgia, and even the Big Island of Hawaii, where Volcano Winery sits at the 4,000-foot level on the slopes of Mauna Loa crater.[2]

Then there are the more familiar hazards of grape growing—pests. "The troubles begin literally at ground level," reported the *San Francisco Chronicle* in 1994, as news spread that acres of vineyards in Napa Valley were dying from phylloxera, a root louse that had mutated so it can attack formerly resistant rootstocks. The ancient pest had long haunted vineyards in Europe and the United States. "We don't have phylloxera here" in Santa Barbara County, Stephan Bedford said in early 1995, "but we do have oak root fungus, nematodes, and mineral toxicity." He was right, but not for long.

Two years earlier, wine writer Clive Irving reported that "a serpent is slowly advancing toward this Eden—or, rather, a bug. It's a nasty greenish yellow insect called phylloxera." It arrived—or broke into the news—in July 1995: "Ballard Vineyard Beset by Phylloxera," announced the *Santa Barbara News-Press*, reporting a Santa Ynez Valley infestation—the first recorded in the region.[3]

History reminded us that French vineyards had been devastated by the louse but were successfully replanted, and that Bay Area vineyards had the same experience late in the nineteenth century. Phylloxera was beatable, Firestone's president Adam Firestone told reporters: "We're not panicking and we're certainly not doomed. We have to take aggressive measures now,

[but] we have a lot of factors in our favor." Weakened vines would be destroyed, resistant stock would be planted, vehicles would be washed. "This bug inevitably gets to everyone" in the grape-growing business, said Jim Wolpert, chairman of the University of California Phylloxera Task Force. Vineyards can be replanted, however, and flourish again.[4]

Another issue affecting the wine industry is that of wine's health effects, which thrust itself into view in the 1980s and 1990s when the public was told to be wary of many accepted foods. Wine had a long history of medicinal uses, but in the second half of the twentieth century, Americans' passionate concern for personal well-being brought critical attention to commodities such as tobacco, liquor, eggs, bacon—and wine. Congress enacted the Alcohol Labeling Amendment in the Anti-Drug Law of 1988, requiring health warnings by 1990 on wine sold in the United States. The media in 1991 also carried stories about alleged health effects of leaded foil capsules used over wine bottle corks.

The brief flare-up about whether wine might be unhealthy was soon neutralized and even reversed. In November 1991, CBS's "Sixty Minutes" presented a report on what was being called "the French Paradox," medical evidence that daily, moderate intake of red wine seemed to lower the rate of heart disease. The French had high-fat diets, but suffered much less

heart disease than Americans. The study attributed this to the French consumption of red wine, which may either elevate HDL (the "good cholesterol") levels in the blood, or contribute useful antioxidants, or both. In 1992 the sales of red wine went up 33 percent, reversing a downward trend that had been cutting red wine sales by 4.5 percent from 1980 to 1990. A 1995 study in Denmark confirmed the beneficial effects of moderate wine drinking while extending the definition of moderate consumption to nearly a bottle per day.[5]

REACHING THEIR STRIDE

*I*n the United States and abroad, the history of wine tells us that grape growing and winemaking migrate, that many people try to learn the art of viniculture, and that some succeed. But the assets of California in general and the Santa Barbara region in particular will be very hard to match. Here in the Santa Maria and Santa Ynez Valleys, the growing seasons are long, providing an average of 125 to 140 days for grapes to ripen as compared to 100 to 105 days in Burgundy, where autumn rains force the harvest. Northern California vineyards receive more intense heat than those in Santa Barbara, so the northern grapes ripen quickly with some loss of acidity. Slower and longer ripening produces better fruit and, in the right hands, better wines. The climate invites

infinite experiments in matching vines with well-drained soils and innumerable slopes, ridges, and bottomland at varying distances from the cooling sea. The combination of climate, shelter from the wind, drainage, and sun is captured by the French word *terroir*. In Santa Barbara County grape growers enjoy a very favorable *terroir*, enticing

☙ TOP: BOB LINDQUIST (QUPÉ) AND JIM CLENDENEN (AU BON CLIMAT) HAVE SHARED WINERY FACILITIES SINCE 1982.
BOTTOM: CHRIS WHITCRAFT HAS PRODUCED LIMITED AMOUNTS OF CHARDONNAY AND PINOT NOIR SINCE 1985.

᠁ TOP: BABCOCK VINEYARDS, ALONG WITH SWEENEY CANYON AND HUBER VINEYARDS, ARE LOCATED IN ONE OF THE COUNTY'S COOLEST GRAPE-GROWING AREAS, NEAR LOMPOC. BOTTOM: MERIDIAN VINEYARDS, WHOSE WINERY IS IN PASO ROBLES, HAS BECOME KNOWN FOR SANTA BARBARA COUNTY WINES MADE FROM GRAPES GROWN IN THEIR VINEYARDS IN LOS ALAMOS AND SANTA MARIA.

combinations of microclimates meeting earth, in one of the longest growing seasons in the state.[6]

Writer Vicki Leon described this region as a "soft land whose shoulders are vine-velveted, oak-dotted, [and] fog-nourished," and *Conde Nast Traveler* foresaw the area's future as "the equal of any winemaking region in the world."[7] If anything threatened that future it was more than a tiny insect. The history of California's wine regions suggests that the ultimate threat is not a bug that can be combatted with science and hard work, but rather the population-driven urban sprawl that now threatens to end the great days of Napa and Sonoma counties. "Every year the bulldozers...swallow up several hundred thousand acres of once green countryside for new suburbs, new shopping centers and new highways," the *New York Times* said of Napa Valley—in 1965! The paper reported that repeated efforts to control growth in that narrow valley and neighboring Sonoma have only slowed their transformation into places with little room for the vines between the subdivisions, increasingly too crowded to entice those attracted to the rural experience of wine tasting.[8] Napa Valley traffic jams have led to a railroad alternative to the main highway for wine country visitors. Sonoma County's growing pains, according to the *San Francisco Chronicle*, are driven by an influx of population that will push the county's

total to half a million people by the year 2006.[9] The long-term challenge to the custodians of Santa Barbara County's grape-growing regions is to manage and limit urban sprawl.

Everyone we talked to in the wine industry is aware of this long-term agenda, as they concentrate upon the grapes ripening on the vines this year, and making this year's vintage even better than the last. "The feeling

᠁ THE BARREL ROOM AT THE GAINEY VINEYARD IS PART OF THE WINERY TOUR.

among insiders," concluded Irving after his first visit to the region, "is that there is a mother lode of some kind hidden here in the complex microclimates and the cocktail of soils." The area's winemakers "feel they have barely hit their stride." The South Central Coast, in the word of journalist Jeff Morgan, "is poised for significant growth as well as glory." Vicki Leon came away from her conversations with local winemakers with the same impression: "The best is yet to come."[10] ᠁

Wine Tasting Tours in Santa Barbara County

A thorough tour of Santa Barbara's wine country would entail several days and take you through some of central California's most picturesque farmland. Fortunately, the county's wine region easily lends itself to shorter tours that range from a few hours to a full day. Many wineries are located near major highways and several areas contain clusters of tasting rooms, which allow you to sample from three or four vintners without driving long distances.

Call the Santa Barbara County Vintners' Association's convenient toll-free number (1-800-218-0881) for a current wine touring map or pick one up at a local winery, hotel, or visitor center.

If you divide the area along geographic lines, six possible itineraries present themselves:

1. Buellton-Lompoc loop: Along this route you can visit Mosby Winery, Sanford Winery, Babcock Vineyards, and Arthur Earl.

2. Santa Ynez/Ballard: Begin your tour in historic Santa Ynez and end in the little township of Ballard, with tasting stops at The Gainey Vineyard, Santa Ynez Winery, Sunstone Vineyards and Winery, Buttonwood Farm Winery, and Foley Estates Vineyard and Winery.

3. Los Olivos area: This route takes you west from Santa Ynez through Los Olivos with visits to Beckmen Vineyards, Brander Vineyard, Los Olivos Vintners, and Rusack Vineyards.

4. Foxen Canyon /Alisos Canyon roads: Proceeding north from Los Olivos along scenic Foxen Canyon Road to Alisos Canyon Road takes you to Firestone Vineyard, Fess Parker Winery, Andrew Murray Vineyards (by appointment), Zaca Mesa Winery, and Bedford-Thompson Winery.

5. East on Betteravia Road from Santa Maria: Driving east along Betteravia Road allows you to make tasting stops at Cottonwood Canyon Vineyard, Cambria Winery, Byron Winery, Rancho Sisquoc Winery, and Foxen Vineyard.

6. City of Santa Barbara: Although there are no commercial vineyards within the city limits, Santa Barbara Winery's winemaking facility and tasting room and Stearns Wharf Vintners' tasting room are convenient stops.

Most wineries are located close together enough to allow you to mix and match locations from the tours above. There are also private tasting rooms in Los Olivos, Solvang, and Santa Barbara that feature wines produced by winemakers without tasting rooms.

Wine tasting tips: Appoint a designated driver or take a guided tour. Eat and drink water as you go. Pack or purchase a picnic lunch and carry a bottle of water. If you are visiting several wineries, focus on one or two varietals to taste and compare, rather than trying to experience every wine offered at every tasting room.

✎ A ROAD WINDS THROUGH VINEYARDS IN THE SANTA YNEZ VALLEY.

Wineries and Vineyards
(June 1997)

1   Andrew Murray Vineyards, 1990†
2   Arroyo Perdido Vineyard (Evergreen), 1974
3   Arthur Earl, 1996†
4   AVC Vineyard (formerly Austin Vineyard), 1992
5   Babcock Vineyards, 1980†
** Barnwood Vineyards, 1984†
6   Beckmen Vineyards (formerly Houtz Vineyards), 1982†
7   Bedford Thompson Winery & Vineyard/
    Thompson Vineyard, 1990†
8   Bien Nacido Vineyards, 1972†
9   Blackjack Vineyards, 1996
10 The Brander Vineyard, 1975†
11 Burning Creek Ranch, 1997
12 Buttonwood Farm Winery & Vineyard, 1983†
13 Byron Vineyard & Winery, 1964 (includes Nielson,
    Fesler, East Mesa, Tepusquet, and Rowan vineyards)†
14 Cambria Winery & Vineyards, 1971
    (includes part of former Tepusquet Vineyard)†
15 Careaga Canyon Ranch & Vineyard
    (Stephens Vineyard), 1989†
16 Carhartt Vineyard, 1996
17 Carrari Vineyard – Rancho don Miguel, 1979
    Rancho Santa Felicia, 1952
    Vista del Valle, 1974
18 Casa Blanca Vineyard (formerly Douglas Vineyard), 1972
19 Cat Canyon Vineyard, 1980
20 Chimère, 1989†
21 Clos Pepe, 1996†
22 Cottonwood Canyon Vineyard & Winery, 1988†
23 Curtis Winery, 1995†
24 Daly Vineyard (formerly Forthman), 1981†
25 East Valley Vineyard, 1978
26 Eleven Oaks Ranch, 1980
27 Fess Parker Winery & Vineyard, 1989†
*   Fiddlehead Cellars, 1989†
28 Firestone Vineyard, 1975†
29 Foley Estates Vineyard & Winery
    (formerly J. Carey Cellars), 1974†
30 Foxen Vineyard and Tinaquaic Vineyard, 1987†
31 The Gainey Vineyard, 1984†
32 The Gainey Vineyard #2, 1997
33 Geoffrey Cellars, 1976
34 Gold Coast Vineyard, 1989
35 Goodchild/Lucas Vineyard, 1993†
36 Harmon Family Vineyards, 1997†
37 Hilltop Vineyard, 1980
38 Huber Vineyard, 1988†
*   Jaffurs Wine Cellars, 1994†
39 JK Vineyard, 1990†
40 Kingsley Vineyard (formerly Adobe Canyon), 1980†
41 La Presa Vineyard, 1974
42 Lafond Vineyard, 1972
*   Lane Tanner Winery, 1989†
43 Lewellen & Lucas Vineyard (St. Jude's), 1977†

44 Los Olivos Vintners (formerly Austin Cellars), 1981†
45 Marcella's Vineyard (form. part of Sierra Madre), 1972
*   McKeon-Phillips Winery, 1982†
46 Melville Vineyards, 1997†
** Meridian Vineyards, 1988†
47 Mission Trails Vineyard, 1996
48 Morehouse & Rothberg Vineyard, 1992†
*   Morovino, 1994†
49 Mosby Vineyard, 1977†
50 Mt. Carmel Vineyards, 1984†
51 North Canyon Vineyard (formerly Newhall), 1971
52 Northwood Los Alamos Vineyards, 1972
*   Presidio Winery, 1992†
53 Qupé/Au Bon Climat, 1982†
54 Rancho El Jabali and Sanford Winery, 1981†
55 Rancho Los Alamos, 1996
56 Rancho Ontiveros Vineyard, 1995
57 Rancho Sisquoc, 1968†
58 Rancho Vinedo, 1973
59 Riverbench Vineyard, 1970s
60 Rozak Ranch Vineyard, 1994†
61 Rusack Vineyards (formerly Ballard Canyon
    Winery), 1975†
62 Sanford & Benedict Vineyard (Talinda Oaks), 1971
63 Santa Barbara Winery, 1962†
64 Santa Maria Hills Vineyard, 1973
65 Santa Rita Vineyard, 1997†

66 Santa Ynez Winery, 1975†
67 Savanna Vineyard, 1973
68 Scott Vineyard, 1981
69 SF Ranch (formerly Braun Vineyard), 1974
70 Sierra Madre Vineyard, 1972
71 Stearns Wharf Vintners, 1965†
72 Stolpman Vineyard, 1992†
73 Sunstone Vineyards and Winery, 1989†
74 Sutter Home Vineyard, 1996
75 Sweeney Canyon Vineyard, 1980†
76 Valley Oaks Vineyard (Ibarra-Young), 1974
77 Valley View Vineyard (formerly
    Ott Vineyard), 1974†
78 Vandale Vineyard, 1991†
79 Vega Vineyard and Mosby Winery, 1971
80 Vina de Santa Ynez, 1969
81 Westerly Vineyards, 1996
*   Whitcraft Winery, 1985†
82 White Gate Ranch, 1981
83 White Hawk Vineyard, 1996†
84 White Hills Vineyard, 1979
85 Wilkening Vineyard, 1981
86 Zaca Mesa Winery, 1973π†

---

*   No visitor facilities   ** Outside map area
†   Member, Santa Barbara County
    Vintners' Association as of June 1997

Dates refer to first vineyard or winery activity at the site

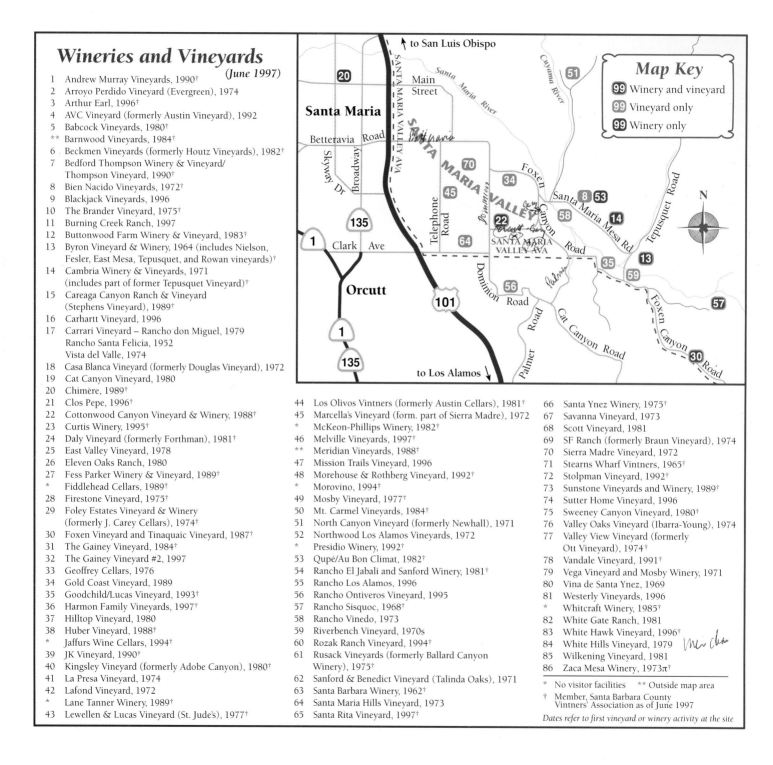

to San Luis Obispo

Santa Maria

Main Street

Betteravia Road

Skyway Dr

Broadway

135

1

Clark Ave

Orcutt

101

1

135

to Los Alamos

Santa Maria River

SANTA MARIA VALLEY AVA

SANTA MARIA VALLEY

Telephone Road

Dominion Road

Foxen Canyon Road

SANTA MARIA VALLEY AVA

Cuyama River

Santa Maria Mesa Rd

Tepusquet Road

Palmer Road

Cat Canyon Road

Foxen Canyon Road

N

Map Key
99 Winery and vineyard
99 Vineyard only
99 Winery only

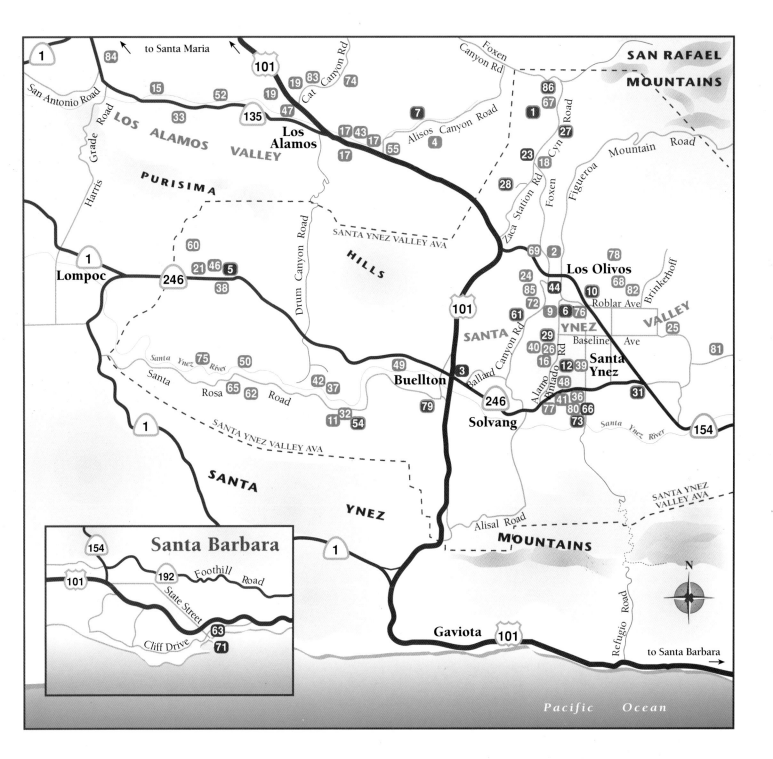

SANTA BARBARA COUNTY VINTNERS' ASSOCIATION MEMBERS

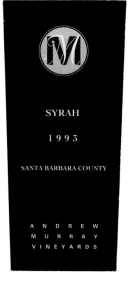

ANDREW MURRAY VINEYARDS

Andrew Murray Vineyards is the only estate in Santa Barbara County to focus exclusively on Rhone varietals, with 35 acres of Syrah, Viognier, Roussanne, Grenache, Mourvedre, and Marsanne all growing on steep hillsides at an elevation of 1,500 feet. The estate winery was fashioned after a French country manor, complete with aromatic Provençal gardens and terraces with breathtaking views of the hillside vineyards and surrounding mountains. The family invites you to taste their handmade wines and to share in their dream of producing the world's finest Rhone varietal wines.

ARTHUR EARL

Opened in 1996, Arthur Earl is a "city winery" located near the freeway in Buellton. The spacious warehouse facility has been transformed into a full-function winery with a tasting room and tours available. Ample space also allows for social events within a convenient distance of hotels and major roadways. While there are no grapes to be seen at the winery, the grapes crushed by Arthur Earl are selected from the best available in Santa Barbara County and the Central Coast. Arthur Earl produces dry white, dry red, and sweet wines in both silver label and gold label releases.

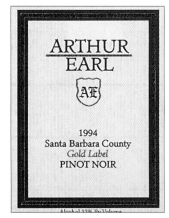

BABCOCK VINEYARDS

In 1978, dentist Walt Babcock and his wife, Mona, owners of Walts' Wharf restaurant in Seal Beach, bought 110 acres of land on the cool western edge of the Santa Ynez Valley. They soon discovered the land was ideal for grapes and subsequently planted 50 acres of vineyards. Bryan Babcock, their son, has been winemaker since the winery's inception in 1984. He has since accumulated numerous awards and accolades for his premium handcrafted wines. Bryan was the only American winemaker chosen as one of the "Top Ten Small Production Winemakers in the World" at a James Beard Foundation event in New York City. Bottlings include spectacular single vineyard Chardonnays and Pinot Noirs, "Eleven Oaks" Sauvignon Blanc and Sangiovese, estate-grown Riesling and Gewurztraminer, Syrah, and experiments in Albarino, Tempranillo, Pignolo, and Pinot Gris.

BARNWOOD VINEYARDS

Barnwood Vineyards is nestled in the foothills of the Cuyama Valley, 42 miles northwest of Ojai in Santa Barbara County at the intersection of Quatal Canyon and Highway 33. Follow the cobblestone driveway to the Main House, which is built out of aged and weathered barnwood. Barnwood Vineyards was the first to grow wine grapes on a commercial basis in the Cuyama Valley of Santa Barbara County. Set in a picturesque location of mesas and rolling hills, the vineyards are planted at 3,200 feet above sea level and overlook the southern end of the valley.

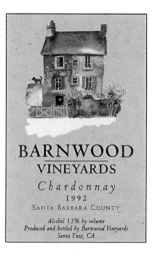

BECKMEN VINEYARDS

The Beckmen family proudly debuted their first release at the 1995 "Celebration of Harvest." Current production includes Sauvignon Blanc, Chardonnay, and Cabernet Sauvignon, with future plans for Syrah, Merlot, and Muscat. They invite you to visit their rustic winery in Los Olivos. Surrounded by vineyards, you can relax under one of the gazebos by the pond and enjoy a bottle of wine. Winemaker: Steve Beckmen.

BEDFORD THOMPSON WINERY & VINEYARD

Although it was established in 1993, Bedford Thompson Winery & Vineyard offers Old World elegance. Tucked away under old oaks and pines, a small rustic farmhouse and barn serve as tasting room and winery. Time-honored winemaking techniques produce the highest quality wines of distinctive character, emphasizing varietal integrity coupled with the inherent properties of an extraordinary vineyard. Vineyard owner David Thompson farms 35 acres of estate vines located on steep, south-facing hills in the Los Alamos Valley. The Thompson Vineyard is planted to Chardonnay, Syrah, and Cabernet Franc, with low yields and cool (Region 1) growing conditions providing superb fruit. Stephan Bedford is winemaker with 20 years of experience.

THE BRANDER VINEYARD

The planting of The Brander Vineyard to mainly Bordeaux varietals began in 1975. In 1977, the first harvest of Sauvignon Blanc grapes was taken to a neighboring winery where Fred Brander produced a wine so distinctive it captured Santa Barbara County's first gold medal at a major wine competition at the Los Angeles County Fair. Since its inception, The Brander Vineyard has been highly acclaimed as a top producer of Sauvignon Blanc, which for many years was the only Brander wine. Today, however, the winery produces an average of 8,000 cases of estate wine from its 40-acre vineyard in the Santa Ynez Valley. Along with its Sauvignon Blanc (blended with Semillon), it also produces Bouchet (a blend of red Bordeaux varietals) and a small quantity of Chardonnay.

BUTTONWOOD FARM WINERY

When Buttonwood Farm Winery started making wine in 1989, they were fortunate to acquire as winemaker someone with a "past." By the time Michael Brown arrived at Buttonwood, he had already sharpened his vinicultural skills at a handful of wineries throughout Santa Barbara County. After earning a graduate degree from UC Davis in 1983, Mike took a position with the newly established Los Vineros Vintners. From there he served as Ken Brown's assistant at Zaca Mesa. The native Australian then spent four years as winemaker at the Santa Ynez Winery where he produced many award-winning wines. After a short stint at Mosby and the launching of his own label, Kalyra, Mike came to Buttonwood Farm where, for the past eight years, he has produced Sauvignon Blanc, Merlot, Cabernet Sauvignon, Cabernet Franc, and Marsanne.

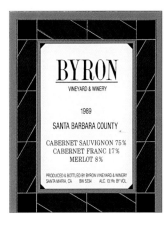

BYRON VINEYARD & WINERY

Byron Vineyard & Winery was founded in 1984 by winemaker/general manager Byron "Ken" Brown, a 20-year veteran of Santa Barbara County winemaking. The winery focuses on Pinot Noir and Chardonnay crafted in the traditional Burgundian style, and produces limited quantities of Pinot Blanc, Pinot Gris, and Sauvignon Blanc. The 640-acre Byron estate includes the oldest commercial vineyard in Santa Barbara County, planted in 1964. Byron also cultivates one of the most extensive experimental vineyards in California, resulting in continual improvement of grape quality. In August 1996, Byron celebrated the completion of a gravity-flow, state-of-the-art winery to ensure uncompromising winemaking quality.

CAMBRIA WINERY & VINEYARD

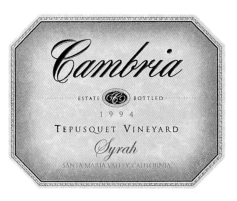

Cambria Winery & Vineyard lies in the Santa Maria Valley, part of an 1838 Mexican land grant known as Rancho Tepusquet. Pioneer grape farmers first planted vines in the area in the early 1970s, and Tepusquet Vineyards subsequently earned a reputation for producing intensely flavorful Chardonnays from the unique soils and microclimates on the Santa Maria Bench. Grape buyers at the time included such wineries as Ridge, Acacia, ZD, Beringer, and Kendall-Jackson. Jess Jackson purchased the Tepusquet Vineyard in 1987 to ensure continued access to the superlative fruit for his Cambria brand. Now known as the Cambria Estate Vineyard, the property is planted to Chardonnay, Pinot Noir, and small amounts of Barbera, Pinot Gris, Sangiovese, Syrah, and Viognier. Stylistically, all the wines reflect the bold, intense fruit character, silky texture, and rich complexity for which Cambria has become known.

CHIMÈRE WINERY

Gary K. Mosby established Chimère Winery in 1989. Mosby received his degree in Food Science and Enology from UC Davis and began his career with Ric Foreman at Sterling Vineyards. He then served as assistant winemaker at Chalone for Dick Graff. Later, Gary established Edna Valley Vineyard. The winery, named after a mythical creature in Greek mythology, produces small quantities of Chardonnay and unfiltered Pinot Noir, as well as Pinot Blanc, Nebbiolo, and Merlot. These handcrafted wines are produced using holistic and traditional techniques. They also avoid over treatment and movement of wine. Here is what wine critics have to say about Chimère wines: Anthony Dias Blue: "(Gary) Mosby never makes wishy-washy wines." Robert Parker: "Chimère is dedicated to producing full-blown, rich unctuous Chardonnays and Pinot Noirs. Impressive wines." Dan Berger: "Gary produces classic style Pinot Noir."

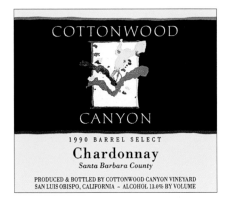

COTTONWOOD CANYON VINEYARD & WINERY

Cottonwood Canyon Vineyard & Winery is the most northern winery in Santa Barbara County. Santa Maria Valley, with its unique microclimate, has become world-famous for Chardonnay and Pinot Noir. Cottonwood Canyon's picturesque 80-acre property abounds with oak and eucalyptus trees in addition to its several cottonwood trees. Norman Beko and his family purchased the vineyard in 1988 because of its ideal location and soil. The Santa Maria Valley is the only wine grape growing region where the ocean is perpendicular to the vineyard, allowing the ocean breeze and fog an unhindered approach to the vineyard. This ocean influence extends the growing season approximately six weeks, yielding small clusters of small berries that give Cottonwood wines their "fruity bouquet and taste."

CURTIS WINERY

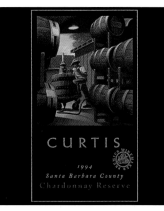

Curtis Winery, owned by the Firestone family, is located in the Foxen Canyon area of the Santa Ynez Valley. Formerly known as Carey Cellars, it was purchased by the Firestones in 1987 and was renamed Curtis in 1995. The facility and vineyards in Solvang were sold in 1997 and the winery was relocated to a contemporary state-of-the-art, gravity-flow facility in Foxen Canyon. Curtis produces small lots of handcrafted, super-premium wines with a focus on Rhone varietals. Winemaker Chuck Carlson sources grapes from mature vineyards where the varietal, soil, and microclimate are perfectly matched. The aim of Curtis Winery is to create wines that capture the essence and diversity that make Santa Barbara County one of the world's greatest wine-growing regions.

FESS PARKER WINERY & VINEYARD

In 1987, Eli Parker (Fess III) and his father purchased a large parcel of rolling ranch land in the Santa Ynez Valley that became the home of their vineyards, their winery, and their families. Eli supervised the planting of the first vines and apprenticed himself to well-known winemaker Jed Steele, who was brought in as a consultant in 1993. The fame of the winery's namesake, known by all for his roles as Davy Crockett and Daniel Boone, is being matched by the accomplishments of his son. Signature wines are Syrah, Pinot Noir, Merlot, Chardonnay, and Johannisberg Riesling. The attractive winery hosts events for up to 2,000 people.

FIDDLEHEAD CELLARS

In 1989, Kathy Joseph created Fiddlehead Cellars specifically to make Santa Barbara County Pinot Noir and Sauvignon Blanc. Attracted to the region for its high-quality fruit and its identifiable *terrior,* Kathy was impressed with the subtle textures, intensity of flavors, and layers of charm extracted from the fruit. Her first vintage of 100 cases of Pinot Noir was rewarded as a selection for the White House table. Kathy continues her commitment to Santa Barbara County with the 1996 purchase of a ranch in the western Santa Ynez Valley, destined to become a close-spaced Pinot Noir vineyard planted in Burgundy clones.

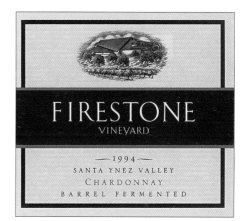

FIRESTONE VINEYARD

Firestone Vineyard was the first commercial winery in the Santa Ynez Valley to produce wine from locally grown grapes. Started in 1972 by Brooks and Kate Firestone, the winery has grown to 540 acres of estate vineyards producing Cabernet Sauvignon, Merlot, Syrah, Sauvignon Blanc, Gewurztraminer, Johannisberg Riesling, and Chardonnay. Winemaker: Alison Green Doran.

FOLEY ESTATES VINEYARD & WINERY

Originally called J. Carey Cellars, and later, Carey Cellars, the winery became Foley Estates Vineyard & Winery in 1997. Foley Estates offers rustic charm in a beautiful country vineyard setting framed by the San Rafael Mountains and features the limited production of handcrafted wines notable for their quality and individuality. Winemaker John Kerr makes a wide variety of wines from both the Foley Estate and many of Santa Barbara County's most noteworthy vineyards.

FOXEN VINEYARD

Bill Wathen and Dick Doré began making wine together in 1985, founding and bonding Foxen Vineyard in 1987. Since then, Foxen has been dedicated to the production of handmade wines using traditional French methods. White wines are all barrel fermented and undergo malo-lactic fermentation. They are aged in French oak barrels, with extensive lees contact, for 10 to 18 months. Red wines are open-top fermented and are aggressively punched down during fermentation. They are pressed off and placed in French oak barrels for 18 to 24 months. A very high percentage of new French oak barrels are used in all wines to balance the high varietal fruit character and the high acid characteristic of the fruit from this appellation. Foxen produces small amounts of six varietals: Chardonnay, Chenin Blanc, Pinot Noir, Cabernet Sauvignon, Merlot, and Cabernet Franc.

THE GAINEY VINEYARD

For over 12 years the Gainey family has been committed to producing premium, handcrafted wines. Located on the northern boundary of the Gainey Ranch in Santa Ynez, The Gainey Vineyard produces 15,000 cases annually, including Chardonnay, Sauvignon Blanc, Johannisberg Riesling, Merlot, Cabernet Franc, and Pinot Noir. The beautiful 12,000-square-foot Spanish-style winery welcomes visitors daily.

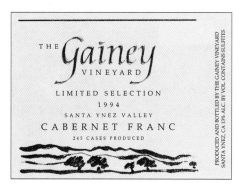

JAFFURS WINE CELLARS

Jaffurs Wine Cellars is dedicated to producing some of the best Rhone varietal wines in the world. Bonded in September 1994, it is one of the newest wineries in the county. Owner/winemaker Craig Jaffurs, working out of the Central Coast Wine Warehouse in Santa Maria, produced his first wines during the 1994 harvest—a Chardonnay and a Syrah. During harvest '95, production increased from 400 to 700 cases, including Syrah, Matilija Cuvée (a Mourvedre-based blend), Grenache, and Chardonnay. In 1996, production rose to 1,400 cases, including the first vintage of Viognier.

LANE TANNER WINERY

Lane Tanner Winery is solely owned and operated by Lane Tanner. Lane came to the wine industry after a few grueling years in environmental science. She started making wine on her own in 1984 and established her winery in 1989. From 1986 to 1996, Lane made only Pinot Noir and only from Santa Barbara County grapes. Pinot Noir is her passion, and her goal has been not to dominate but to finesse the truly feminine characters out of the Pinot Noir grape. She started making other wines in 1996 after a failed Pinot harvest in 1995. She uses the same technique and philosophy with them, but her true love is and will always be Pinot Noir, the queen of the grapes.

LOS OLIVOS VINTNERS/AUSTIN CELLARS

Started in 1981 as Austin Cellars, Los Olivos Vintners was acquired by its current owners in 1992. The original winemaker was Tony Austin, from whom the winery took its name. Today, the winery continues to produce wines under the Austin Cellars label, but Los Olivos Vintners has become their business name and the brand name for their "Reserve" wines. Known for Pinot Noir and dessert wine, in recent years they have achieved great success with their Chardonnay and Cabernet. As one of the wineries whose tasting room is separate from their winery, they have occupied the same building in downtown Los Olivos since 1985.

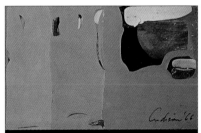

MCKEON-PHILLIPS WINERY

McKeon-Phillips was founded by Susan McKeon and Ardison Phillips in 1982. The excellent wines made by Ardison include Sauvignon Blanc from Santa Ynez Valley grapes, a Pinot Noir from the Santa Maria Valley, and his signature Cabernet Sauvignon and Cabernet Franc, both made exclusively from Daly Vineyard grapes. Ardison's Cabernets, which have earned him numerous gold medals, are uniquely aged using four specific oak barrel types and then equally blended at bottling to provide a rich multilayered complexity, great fruits, and delicate tannins.

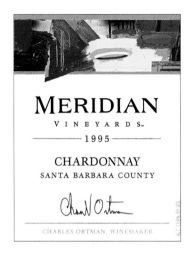

MERIDIAN VINEYARDS

Meridian Vineyards was established in 1988. Although the winery is located in Paso Robles, Meridian has significant vineyard acreage in Santa Barbara County. The label was started in 1984 by Chuck Ortman, a veteran winemaker and consultant from Napa Valley. In 1988, Chuck relocated to San Luis Obispo where he began to produce wines from Santa Barbara County, Edna Valley, and Paso Robles wine appellations. His winemaking philosophy is to guide the fruit to a delicately balanced wine, combining the characteristics from different vineyards to achieve a wine's complexity.

MOROVINO

A veteran of the difficult Olympic decathlon, Santa Barbara vintner Gerry Moro is facing competition of a different sort these days. His quest now is to buy enough grapes for his new Morovino wines. Moro moved to Santa Barbara in 1966 and eventually became a building contractor. Later he befriended Bill Wathen and Dick Doré of Foxen Vineyard. He began to work during crush at Foxen and received wine instead of cash for his efforts. He also jumped at the chance to learn winemaking. The first vintage of Morovino was bottled in 1994, the year Moro decided to invest all of his time establishing himself as a winemaker. He gave up luxuries, rented out his home, and moved into a trailer, living on money he has saved while starting up his winemaking business.

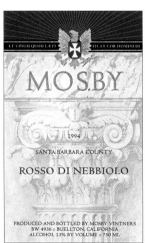

MOSBY WINERY

Mosby Winery is committed to producing lean, sleek wines that stand on their own, yet provide a perfect partnership with food. Today, the winemaking emphasis has broadened to encompass the great Italian wines, including Sangiovese, Nebbiolo, Pinot Grigio, Dolcetto, and several test blocks of other promising varietals. Great success has also been achieved by producing two gold medal distillates: Grappa di Traminer and a Distillation of Wild Plum. Winemaker: Bill Mosby.

PRESIDIO WINES

Presidio Wines produces small lots of handcrafted premium wines under the direction of award-winning winemaker Douglas Braun. His philosophy is to create well-extracted, balanced, and flavorful wines by working from fruit of low-yielding vineyards and controlling every step of the process from vine to bottle. Presidio's wines are aged in French oak barrels and carefully stored in the natural humidity and cool temperatures of stone caves built into the vineyards' hillsides to ensure proper aging and maturing. Braun and co-worker Michael Powers plan to strictly produce quality California wines of good value. Presidio Wines recently acquired 35 acres in Santa Maria of Burgundian varietal producing vines so they could further control the quality of fruit from which their top-rated wines are produced.

QUPÉ /AU BON CLIMAT

Qupé/Au Bon Climat winery is located at the Bien Nacido Vineyard in the northern part of the county. Qupé winemaker Bob Lindquist produces Chardonnay and Rhone varietals. Au Bon Climat produces Chardonnay, Pinot Noir, and Pinot Blanc with Jim Clendenen as winemaker. This co-op facility also produces wines under the Vita Nova, Il Podere, Hitching Post, and Makor labels.

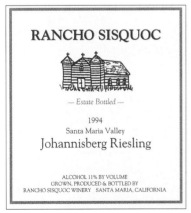

RANCHO SISQUOC WINERY

Located on a 37,000-acre ranch, Rancho Sisquoc beckons back to an earlier, more tranquil era. Overlooking the entrance to the ranch is the historic San Ramon Chapel, which also adorns every label. The unpretentious winery is surrounded by green pastures and fruit trees, an ideal setting for those seeking handcrafted wines and a respite from city life. The winery produces a broad range of wines exclusively from their 208-acre vineyard. Winemaker Carol Botwright enthusiastically looks forward to the future as the ranch celebrates its 25th anniversary of fine winemaking in 1997.

RUSACK VINEYARDS

Newly established Rusack Vineyards is focusing its efforts on handcrafted premium wines ranging from Chardonnay and Riesling to Syrah and Merlot. Proprietors Geoff and Alison Rusack have also created "Soul of the Vine," a unique dessert wine made from Riesling and Muscat grapes frozen after harvest, resulting in a wonderfully light liqueur similar to the famed German "Eis Wein." The setting at Rusack Vineyards is as special as the wines themselves. Building on the tradition of charm and friendliness established by the property's former owners, the Rusacks have preserved many popular features of the winery, including the inviting redwood deck constructed around three beautiful oak trees and situated overlooking the vines.

SANFORD WINERY

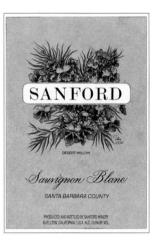

Sanford Winery was established in 1981 by Richard Sanford and his wife, Thekla. One of the early pioneers in the Santa Ynez Valley wine industry, Sanford and his former partner established Sanford & Benedict Vineyard in 1971, and their first wines, from the 1976 vintage, brought attention to the Santa Barbara area, particularly for Pinot Noir. Today, the Sanford Winery and ranch are located in the Santa Ynez Valley five miles west of Buellton. Bruno D'Alfonso became winemaker in 1983, making world-class Pinot Noir, Chardonnay, and Sauvignon Blanc. Distributed worldwide, Sanford wines are produced from grapes grown in several well-established vineyards in Santa Barbara County. The beautiful wildflower labels, a different one for each variety and vintage, are produced each year from original artwork by Sebastian Titus. Visitors are always welcome to visit the tasting room and picnic facility.

SANTA BARBARA WINERY

Established in 1962 as the county's first post-Prohibition winery, Santa Barbara Winery reflects a long tradition of interest in wine. At first, owner Pierre Lafond made wine from purchased fruit, but in 1972 he established Lafond Vineyard in the Santa Ynez Valley with the help of viticulturist Bill Collins. In 1981, Bruce McGuire was hired as winemaker and began producing premium wines. Among them are Beaujour (a light Beaujolais-style Zinfandel meant to be consumed young) and Paradis (a dry white Riesling), as well as Chardonnay, Sauvignon Blanc, Pinot Noir, Syrah, and several late harvest wines. Santa Barbara Winery boasts a distinctive heritage of high-quality production, and a promising future as well. Located just two blocks from the beach in downtown Santa Barbara, the winery tasting room is an inviting stop for tourists.

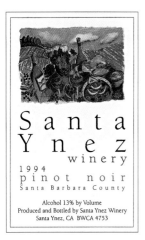

SANTA YNEZ WINERY

Santa Ynez Winery is located on the site of California's first college, El Colegio de Nuestra Senora del Refugio, built in the early 1800s. The winery offers an inviting ranch-style tasting room with a redwood deck that provides a panoramic view of the Santa Ynez Valley. Annual events include barbecues, summer twilight dinners, and an old-fashioned grape stomp harvest party.

STEARNS WHARF VINTNERS

In 1981, Doug and Candy Scott opened Stearns Wharf Vintners tasting room on historic Stearns Wharf in Santa Barbara. Along with the Stearns Wharf Vintners wines, it features tastings from the award-winning Santa Ynez Winery. Come enjoy uncompromising views and a selection of local wines, fresh breads, cheeses, and cappuccino.

SUNSTONE VINEYARDS & WINERY

The Rice family moved to their terraced 55-acre ranch overlooking the Santa Ynez River in 1989. The site was selected for its ideal south-sloping exposure, sandy, rocky soil, and a microclimate well-suited to growing premium wine grapes. Within a year, 25 acres had been planted to Merlot, Cabernet Sauvignon, Syrah, Viognier, and Mourvedre. The goal of owner Fred Rice and winemaker Doug Braun is to produce small lots of exceptionally high-quality, handcrafted estate wines by utilizing organic farming methods and using extensive canopy and crop management techniques. The winery building is reminiscent of those found in the French countryside. A kitchen, complete with a wood-burning oven, is part of the tasting room ambiance, and a stone barrel-aging cave is built into the hillside at the rear of the production room.

WHITCRAFT WINERY

Owner/winemaker Chris Whitcraft founded his winery in 1985 after working ten years as the manager of a fine wine shop. In 1978 he started a series of wine shows on KTMS Radio that aired over 11 years. He also co-founded the Wine Festival at the Santa Barbara Museum of Natural History. In 1978, Chris began making wine with John Graff at Chalone Vineyards, whose influence led Chris toward his focus on Pinot Noir and Chardonnay, as well as his non-interventional winemaking style—using little electricity and never fining, filtering, or pumping the reds. The winery currently leases land from Bien Nacido and contracts grapes from other vineyards. Production is limited, and the wines are available almost exclusively from the winery.

ZACA MESA WINERY

Zaca Mesa Winery is beautifully situated on a 750-acre property in Santa Barbara County's unique transverse mountain corridor. The 224-acre mesa estate vineyard is planted with Chardonnay and the Rhone varietals Syrah, Grenache, Mourvedre, Cinsault, Counoise, Roussanne, and Viognier. In 1978 Zaca Mesa became the first winery in Santa Barbara County to plant Syrah grapes. With winemaker Dan Gehrs at the helm, Zaca Mesa has become a trendsetter with unique Rhone wine blends. Ranking their 1993 Syrah "Number 6" in the world, the *Wine Spectator* acclaimed it as "one of the best Rhone-style wines to come out of California."

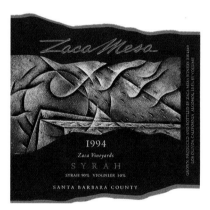

SANTA BARBARA COUNTY VINTNERS' ASSOCIATION: GROWER AND VINEYARD MANAGER/CONSULTANT MEMBERS

All of the wineries profiled above are members of the Santa Barbara County Vintners' Association (SBCVA). The following lists growers and vineyard managers/consultants who are also members of SBCVA as of June, 1997: Bien Nacido Vineyards, Careaga Canyon Ranch & Vineyard, Clos Pepe, Daly Vineyard, Hampton Farming Co., Harmon Family Vineyards, Huber Vineyard, JK Vineyard, Kingsley Vineyard, Lewellen & Lucas Vineyards, Melville Vineyards, Morehouse & Rothberg Vineyard, Mt. Carmel Vineyards, Pacific Vineyard Company, Rozak Ranch Vineyard, Santa Rita Vineyard, Stolpman Vineyard, Sweeney Canyon Vineyard, Vandale Vineyard, and White Hawk Vineyard.

Grape Varieties Grown in Santa Barbara County

Santa Barbara County's many microclimates allow a wide variety of wine grapes to be grown successfully. The area's viticulturists cultivate an impressive array of wine grape varieties, benefitting from a long history of regional experimentation.

WHITE: Of white grape varieties, Chardonnay accounts for by far the most acreage, while there also are substantial plantings of Sauvignon Blanc, White Riesling, Chenin Blanc, and Gewurztraminer. In addition, there are smaller plantings of Muscat Blanc, Muscat Orange, Pinot Blanc, Pinot Gris, Semillon, Sylvaner, and Viognier and new plantings of Albarino, Arneis, and Tocai Fruilano.

RED: Among red grape varieties, Pinot Noir and Cabernet Sauvignon lead the way, followed by Merlot, Syrah, and Cabernet Franc. Smaller acreage is devoted to Barbera, Gamay, Grenache, Mataro, Nebbiolo, Petite Sirah, Roussanne, Sangiovese, and Zinfandel, with additional plantings of Carignan, Malbec, Petite Verdot, Pignolo, Refosco, and Tempranillo.

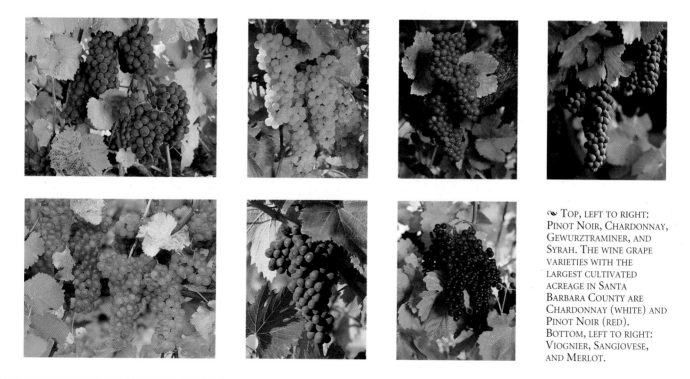

∾ TOP, LEFT TO RIGHT: PINOT NOIR, CHARDONNAY, GEWURZTRAMINER, AND SYRAH. THE WINE GRAPE VARIETIES WITH THE LARGEST CULTIVATED ACREAGE IN SANTA BARBARA COUNTY ARE CHARDONNAY (WHITE) AND PINOT NOIR (RED). BOTTOM, LEFT TO RIGHT: VIOGNIER, SANGIOVESE, AND MERLOT.

APPENDIX 1
WINE: THE LONG JOURNEY TO THE AMERICAS

The culture of wine—grape growing, winemaking, and the enjoyment of wine—travelled a very long way and over many centuries before reaching Santa Barbara County. Grapevines have been found on every continent; over 24,000 varieties of them are named, and 150 varieties are widely used as a source of food. But winemaking—viticulture—was historically localized. The cradle of grape cultivation was apparently in the region of the Caucasus Mountains, between the Black Sea and Caspian Sea. Here, in an area overlapping the contemporary boundaries of Iran, Iraq, and Syria, grew the vine *vitis vinifera,* producer of grapes so well suited to wine that it was fated to be the centerpiece of a world-travelling wine culture. From its origins between 2000 and 6000 B.C., the culture of wine ran outward in channels cut by the expansion of the major religions born in this remarkable crucible of faiths. One of these was Christianity, whose scriptures contained many references to wine and whose savior made wine out of water at a feast and offered it to his disciples at the Last Supper. When Christianity spread north and west out of Palestine, the cultivation of grapes for the making and enjoyment of wine went with it.

Across a range of major civilizations whose achievements shaped our own, wine appears in several roles—as a religious symbol, but also as a medicine and as a libation at ceremonies and meals. It is now known that the world of Islam was not so hostile to wine as religious teachings might imply, and that some viticultural successes may be found on the Arabian peninsula and elsewhere. But the future of wine ran mainly on a northwestern route.

Courses in the history of western civilization take us on a journey out of the eastern Mediterranean through Greece and Rome into Europe. Along that path flowed many human achievements and projects—Christianity itself, the main thrust of the development of science, the seeds of Renaissance humanistic creativity, the emergence of democracy, and the relentless advance of technology. Western technological ingenuity brought into the world some harmful things—gunpowder, the cannon—but also a cascade of useful applied knowledge—navigation, medicine, clockmaking, printing, and making better wine from grapes.

While no archaeologist can tell us for sure, the wines of Italy were said to be superior to the wines of Greece, part of a western thing called progress. After Rome's fall, the art of winemaking was kept alive through the dark centuries by Catholic monks. The wines that were so skillfully made in the river valleys of France and Germany and on the plains of Spain and Portugal could be preserved longer and shipped farther in new cork-capped glass bottles. Wine not only extended its culture to the edge of the Atlantic, but holding its place on the tables of kings, had become a vital part of daily diet, agricultural festivals, and religious rites. And so, in the sixteenth century, wine in casks and bundles of grapevine cuttings travelled in European sailing vessels bound for the New World.

APPENDIX 2
WESTWARD IN SEARCH OF WINE COUNTRY: WINE IN ENGLISH COLONIAL AMERICA

The 13 English colonies had a strong political motive behind their hopes for winemaking from American grapes, if thirst wasn't enough. Under the assumptions of British mercantilism, importing French, Spanish, and Italian wines into England made the British Empire dangerously dependent, and the colonies were under pressure from London to make wine for export back home. The Virginia Company even passed a law in 1619 requiring every householder to plant ten vines yearly, but by mid-century it was painfully evident that even the 10,000 vines planted along the swampy coast of Virginia would lead to wine of dismal quality. Efforts in Florida, South Carolina, Maryland, Pennsylvania, and elsewhere ended in similar failures, whether using native or European varietals.

Even the multitalented genius and dedicated farmer Thomas Jefferson could not produce decent wines at his Monticello estate, despite the help of

Florentine merchant Philip Mazzei, who brought cuttings from Tuscany for a trial in Virginia soil and climate. Brief successes often turned sour. Major John Adlum (1759–1836) took Jefferson's advice and grafted European varietals on native American rootstock at his farm in the Georgetown suburb of Washington, D.C., and was able to ship a tasty Tokay wine to Jefferson and James Madison in the 1820s. Adlum became a sort of national wine guru with his *Adlum on Wine Making,* but after his death in 1836, his own vines succumbed to disease.

By the middle of the nineteenth century, 250 years of European exploration and settlement had probed the northern hemisphere for suitable places to grow grapes. The determination to make good wine from grapes grown in the American garden seemed inexhaustible as the American farmer, ever the optimist, tenaciously experimented to find the right combination of plant, soil, climate, and husbandry.

By trial and error, moving westward across the continent, small regional successes began to accumulate. Nicholas Longworth, Ohio lawyer, horticulturist, and developer, imported European vintners and grafted European varietals to American rootstock for 30 years, and by the 1850s his dry white table wines were acclaimed. German immigrants in New York planted vineyards in 1853, and by the mid-1860s their Hammondsport and Pleasant Valley Wine Company shipped the respected sparkling wines of Jules

Masson to markets outside the state. Perhaps Senator Stephen A. Douglas had not been too optimistic when, in 1851, he announced enthusiastically that "the U.S. will, in a very short time, produce good wine, so cheap, and in such abundance, as to render it a common and daily beverage."

Fortunately, there had also been an accumulation of scientific knowledge and viticultural practices that allowed for those regional successes. For years viticulture had been plagued by ignorance "as growers kept repeating over and over what were, in the circumstances, their futile trials of the vinifera." Yet, governmental and entrepreneurial enthusiasm for an American wine industry never seemed to flag.

Ever so slowly, the industry moved up the learning curve with fairs, exhibitions, and governmental support. Successes in Missouri produced knowledge that would be carried westward. George Husmann, Missouri viticulturist, nurseryman, and writer, compiled "An Essay on the Culture of the Grape in the Great West" (1863), and in his "Cultivation of the Native Grape" and "Manufacture of American Wines" (1866), he addressed the problems of grape growing in western states.

The United States by the mid-nineteenth century seemed finally to have a scattered wine industry born through trial and error and firmly grounded in the latest scientific knowledge. Vintners continued to search for adaptable grape hybrids capable of surviving the country's varied climatic regions and producing

quality juice for wine. Once established, vintners began the process of disseminating information, expanding research, and forming organizations. The Department of Agriculture was created in Washington in 1862, and it established close relations with "land-grant" universities who began to set up experimental stations and departments devoted to viticulture and viniculture. State and local agricultural fairs and exhibitions demonstrated the latest technology and showcased new plant material.

Thus, European settlers persistently experimented with winemaking as they spread westward across the American continent. Yet their spotty success by the mid-1800s still had not found the perfect combination of soil, climate, grape variety, and technique. Little known to these ambitious, struggling wine lovers, Europeans had already found a place where Europe's wines could be matched, or bettered—and that was in Mexico! At least until the War of 1848 it was in Mexico. In that year the state of Alta California was ceded by Mexico to the United States and became the State of California. While stubborn growers toiled in Virginia, New York, Ohio, Missouri, and elsewhere, grapes were planted, harvested, and fermented into wine in a new state with a climate much like that of the Mediterranean— California. Even decades earlier, as Thomas Jefferson brooded among his own vineyards in the late 1700s, Spanish padres had begun to establish vineyards around the developing missions of Alta California.

ENDNOTES

Introduction

[1] The newcomer of 1965 was one of the authors of this book, Otis L. Graham, Jr. The first modern plantings of grapes had gone into the ground the year before.

[2] Gomberg, Fredrikson & Associates, *The Wine Industry's Economic Contribution to Santa Barbara County* (San Francisco: Gomberg, Fredrikson & Associates, 1994), passim.

[3] *California Agriculture Statistical Review 1992* (Sacramento: California Department of Food and Agriculture, 1993); Gomberg, Fredrikson & Associates, *The Wine Industry's Economic Contribution* (San Francisco: Gomberg, Fredrikson & Associates, 1997), passim.

CHAPTER 1

[1] Accounts of the date vary, but the best analysis indicates that Mission grapes arrived over a decade after the first missions were established. Earlier writers, like J. N. Bowman, indicate arrival of grapes before 1782, but Roy Brady has researched this topic thoroughly and believes that the later date is accurate. See comments in Doris Muscatine, Maynard A. Amerine, and Bob Thompson, eds., *The University of California/Sotheby Book of California Wine* (Los Angeles: University of California Press, 1984), 10-15.

[2] J. N. Bowman, "Vineyards of Provincial California," *Wine Review* (May 1943), 16.

[3] Sir George Simpson, *An Overland Journey Round the World, During the Years 1841 and 1842* (Philadelphia: Lee and Blanchard, 1847), 218.

[4] Bowman, "Vineyards of Provincial California," 10.

[5] Mary Louise Days, "Mission Vineyards and San Jose Vineyard: A Relic of Mission Times" (unpublished paper, June 13, 1986).

[6] When twentieth-century preservationists restored La Purísima Concepción, they found grapes believed to be descendants of the padre's plantings, and cuttings from these vines now thrive in a number of historic mission gardens.

[7] Richard S. Whitehead and Mary Louise Days, "San Jose Winery: A Landmark of Old Mission Times," in Gary B. Coombs, ed., *Those Were the Days: Landmarks of Old Goleta* (Goleta, Calif.: Institute for American Research, 1986), 81.

[8] Ernest Peninou and Sidney Greenleaf, *A Directory of California Wine Growers and Wine Makers in 1860* (Berkeley: Tamalpais Press, 1967), 46-47.

[9] Ibid., 46.

[10] Ruth Teiser and Catherine Harroun, *Wine Making in California* (New York: McGraw-Hill, 1983), 17.

[11] Bowman, "Vineyards of Provincial California," 14.

[12] Peninou and Greenleaf *(A Directory of California Wine Growers),* who compiled the estimates from census records, suggest in their preface that the state total is too low. The census reported 246,000 gallons of wine produced in 1860, with Los Angeles producing 150,000 gallons. However, the U.S. Census for 1850 reported California production at 58,055 gallons, although Edwin Bryant, in "What I Saw In California" (1848), states that total production was 1,600,000 gallons in 1847. Bryant exaggerated, but the census predictions are almost certainly too low. Vincent P. Carosso, *The California Wine Industry 1803-1895: A Study of the Formative Years* (Berkeley: University of California Press, 1951), 7-8.

[13] Ibid.

[14] Teiser and Harroun, *Wine Making in California,* 66-67.

[15] Muscatine, Amerine, and Thompson, *University of California/Sotheby Book of Wine,* 8.

[16] California State Board of Agriculture, *Report of the State Board of Agriculture* (Sacramento: 1911), 184.

17 Teiser and Harroun, *Wine Making in California*, 101.

18 Muscatine, Amerine, and Thompson, *University of California/Sotheby Book of Wine*, 558-559. In their Wine Glossary, they define viticulture as the science of winemaking and viniculture as the science of grape growing.

19 Peninou and Greenleaf, *A Directory of California Wine Growers*, 46-47.

20 Stella Rouse, "1865 was a vintage year for Santa Barbara winery," *Santa Barbara News-Press*, 11 October 1986, B-5.

21 Whitehead and Days, *Those Were the Days: Landmarks of Old Goleta*, 85-86.

22 "Olden days: pioneer settler tried many crops," *Santa Barbara News-Press*, 14 September 1969.

23 Board of State Viticultural Commissioners, *Directory of the Grape Growers, Wine Makers and Distillers* (Sacramento: State of California, 1891), 130-131.

24 H. H. Bancroft, *The Works of Hubert Howe Bancroft, Volume XXXIV, California Pastoral 1769-1848* (San Francisco: History Company, 1888), 194.

25 Jesse D. Mason, *History of Santa Barbara County, California* (Oakland: Thompson and West, 1993), 422.

26 Ibid., 301.

27 Helen Caire, *Santa Cruz Island: A History and Recollection of an Old California Rancho* (Spokane: The Arthur H. Clark Company, 1993), passim.

28 George V. Castagnola, interviews with Marian Ashby Johnson for the Santa Barbara Historical Society, 1981-82.

Chapter 2

1 Muscatine, Amerine, and Thompson, *University of California/Sotheby Book of Wine*, 383; Thomas Pinney, *A History of Wine in America from the Beginnings to Prohibition* (Los Angeles: University of California Press, 1989), 374.

2 Muscatine, Amerine, and Thompson, *University of California/Sotheby Book of Wine*, 414, 419.

3 Charles M. Gidney, *History of Santa Barbara, San Luis Obispo and Ventura Counties* (Chicago: The Lewis Publishing Co., 1917), 128. Gidney writes that Lompoc's deed provided that: "No vinous, malt, spirituous, or other intoxicating liquors shall ever be sold or manufactured upon any portion of the Lompoc and Mission Vieja Ranchos purchased by this corporation." A thriving home-winemaking community, however, existed in the Lompoc area for many years.

4 Leon D. Adams, *The Wines of America* (New York: McGraw-Hill, 1985), 23.

5 Muscatine, Amerine, and Thompson, *University of California/Sotheby Book of Wine*, 52.

6 James T. Lapsley, *Bottled Poetry: Napa Winemaking from Prohibition to the Modern Era* (Los Angeles: University of California Press, 1996), 24.

7 Ibid., 7-21.

8 Robert Rossi, "Post-Repeal Wine Consumption," *Wines and Vines* (January 1935), 3.

9 Beverly J. Schwartzberg memo from Wine History Project Files, 15 April and 27 July 1995; Annette Burden, "Pride of the Valley," *Santa Barbara Magazine* (November-December 1983), 40; "Two Goletans' death opens Fiesta," *Santa Barbara News-Press*, 28 August 1931. The 1931 article reported that Orlando Dardi was overcome by fumes on his ranch three miles from Goleta while "punching down the cap" of grape skins that develops atop wine vats during fermentation, and his 20-year-old daughter Lina also died in an effort to rescue him.

10 Lapsley, *Bottled Poetry*, 85-88.

11 Muscatine, Amerine, and Thompson, *University of California/Sotheby Book of Wine*, 78-79; Teiser and Harroun, *Wine Making in California*, Chapter 20.

12 Matt Kramer, *Making Sense of California*

Wines (New York: William Morrow, 1992), 35.

[13] Muscatine, Amerine, and Thompson, *University of California/Sotheby Book of Wine,* 69.

[14] Hugh Johnson, *Vintage: The Story of Wine* (New York: Simon and Schuster, 1989), 452.

[15] Frank J. Prial, "Wine Talk: A coda to the 1976 France vs. California rivalry that changed some attitudes," *New York Times,* 22 May 1996, B-5; "1976 California Stuns France in Parisian Wine Tasting," *Wine Spectator* (30 April 1996, vol. 21 no. 1), 52.

Chapter 3

[1] Muscatine, Amerine, and Thompson, *University of California/Sotheby Book of Wine,* 78-81.

[2] Ibid.

[3] Stanley Hill, interview with Teddy Gasser, 10 January 1987 (interview in the collection of the Santa Barbara Historical Society).

[4] Interview with Craig Addis, Pierre Lafond, Bruce McGuire, and Laila Rashid by Beverly Schwartzberg on 28 January 1994.

[5] "Tepusquet climate ideal for grapes,"

Santa Barbara News-Press, 30 September 1969, A-6.

[6] PG&E report found in the personal files of Dale Hampton.

[7] Bill Griggs, "First S.Y.V. grape harvest proves to be bumper crop," *Santa Barbara News-Press,* 23 October 1973, B-4; Interview with Boyd Bettencourt conducted in Santa Ynez, California by Beverly Schwartzberg on 8 April 1994.

[8] Interview with Ed Holt and Harold Pfeiffer by Richard P. Ryba, 12 April 1995.

[9] Interview with Stephan Bedford by Victor W. Geraci, 24 February 1994.

[10] Interview with Bob and Jeanne Woods, by Richard P. Ryba, 12 April 1995; Interview with Stephan Bedford by Victor W. Geraci, 24 February, 1994.

[11] Interview with Louis Lucas by Richard P. Ryba, 29 June 1994; Interview with Dale Hampton by Victor W. Geraci and Susan Goldstein, 10 February 1994; Dale Hampton, "Napa Valley Grape Trip," report in the Dale Hampton Papers, dated 8-16 August 1970.

[12] Dale Hampton Papers, 8-16 August 1970, 1-4.

[13] Interview with Geraldine Mosby by Susan Goldstein, 28 January 1994.

[14] Robert Lawrence Balzer, *The Los Angeles Times Book of California Wines* (New York: Harry N. Abrams, Inc., 1984), 14; Interview with Richard Sanford by Otis L. Graham, Jr. and Victor W. Geraci, 7 March 1995; Richard P. Hinkle, "Searching for the Holy Grail," *Wines and Vines* (July 1993), passim.

[15] Interview with T. Hayer by Richard P. Ryba, 29 June 1994.

[16] Bank of America, *California Wine Outlook: An Economic Study of the California Wine and Wine Grape Industries,* (San Francisco: Bank of America, September 1973), 3, 17.

[17] Interview with Ed Holt and Harold Pfeiffer by Richard P. Ryba, 21 April 1995. Philip Hiaring, "Miracle at Tepusquet," *Wines and Vines* (November 1971), 21.

[18] Interview with Bob Miller by Richard P. Ryba, 15 September 1994.

[19] Interview with Stephan Bedford by Victor W. Geraci, 24 February 1994.

[20] Interview with A. Brooks Firestone by Richard P. Ryba, 18 February 1995; Interview with Hayley Firestone Jessup by Victor W. Geraci, 3 February 1994; Interview with Geraldine Mosby by Susan Goldstein, 28 January 1994; Frank J. Prial, "A winery in the making," *New York Times,* 23 July 1978.

21 At that time, 34 states reported bonded commercial wineries, and California was the home of 258 of the nation's 446 wineries.

22 California Agricultural Statistics Service, "Statistical Survey of 1972" (May 1973), "Statistical Survey of 1973" (April 1974), "Crop and Crush" (April 1975), *California Wine Grape Acreage* (Sacramento: California Department of Agriculture).

23 Bank of America, *California Wine Outlook*, 3, 17.

24 "Grape grower making wine to avoid economic squeeze," *Santa Barbara News-Press*, 15 September 1985, A-1, A-9.

25 Interview with Doug Scott by Beverly J. Schwartzberg, 10 February 1994; Interview with Fred Brander by Beverly J. Schwartzberg, 16 February 1994; Interview with Boyd and Claire Hunt Bettencourt by Beverly J. Schwartzberg, 8 April 1994.

26 Interview with Byron (Ken) Brown by Richard P. Ryba, 14 September 1994.

27 Interview with Kate Firestone by Victor W. Geraci, 3 February 1994.

28 Interview with Louis Lucas by Richard P. Ryba, 29 June 1994; oral history of A. J. Winkler in the Bancroft, California Oral History Project, University of California, Berkeley.

29 Interview with Stephan Bedford by Victor W. Geraci, 24 February 1995.

30 Hugh Johnson and Bob Thompson, *The California Wine Book* (New York: William Morrow, 1976), 122.

31 *New York Times*, 23 July 1978; *Santa Barbara News-Press*, 2 February 1993; *Los Angeles Times*, 9 August 1990; and Austin Cellars press kit.

32 Bob Thompson, *California Wine Country* (Menlo Park, Calif.: Lane Books, 1969, 1977, 1979), passim; Balzer, *The Los Angeles Times Book of California Wines*, passim.

Chapter 4

1 The basic data and analysis on wine industry trends are the annual statistical surveys in *Wines and Vines*, the economic reports in *Wine Institute News*, and *Jobson's Wine Marketing Handbook*, based on their data for the 1980s.

2 Gomberg, Fredrikson & Associates, *The Wine Industry's Economic Contribution to Santa Barbara County*, (San Francisco: Gomberg, Fredrikson & Associates, 1994), 1-3; Jay Stuller and Glen Martin, *Through the Grapevine* (New York: Wynwood Press, 1989), 24; Kirby Moulton, "The Changing Face of the Wine Economy," *Wine Institute News* (September 1991), 6-7.

3 Mark Schneipp, *Santa Barbara Economic Outlook* (Santa Barbara: University of California Santa Barbara), April 1990, 38, and June 1985, 26-27. See also California Agricultural Statistics Service, *California Wine Grape Acreage* (Sacramento: California Department of Agriculture); Gomberg, Fredrikson & Associates, *The Wine Industry's Economic Contribution to Santa Barbara County*, 3; *Santa Barbara News-Press*, 11 September 1986, 27 September 1987, 14 November 1988, 23 August 1990, 14 April 1991, and 12 April 1994.

4 "Wineries warned on more planting," *Santa Barbara News-Press*, 30 June 1978. Interview with Harold Pfeiffer by Richard P. Ryba, 12 April 1995; Interview with Dale Hampton by Victor W. Geraci and Susan Goldstein, 10 February 1994.

5 "Wines and Vines Revisits Santa Barbara Wine Country," *Wines and Vines* (April 1991), 30.

6 Interview with Dale Hampton by Victor W. Geraci and Susan Goldstein, 10 February 1994; Interview with Stephan Bedford by Victor W. Geraci, 24 February 1994.

7 Gomberg, Fredrickson & Associates, *The Wine Industry's Contribution*, 1994, 2-3.

8 Interview with Jim Clendenen by Richard P. Ryba, 10 February 1994.

9 Interview with Dale Hampton by Victor W. Geraci and Susan Goldstein, 10 February 1994.

[10] Interview with Stephan Bedford by Victor W. Geraci, 24 February 1994.

[11] Wine Institute, *Economic Research Report* (San Francisco: Wine Institute), 15 July 1985 and October 1992, passim.

[12] Richard P. Ryba, "Up from the Cellar: Austin Cellars in the 1990s" (Seminar Biosketch, University of California Santa Barbara, 1995), passim.

[13] Interview with Fess Parker by Victor W. Geraci, 17 April 1995; Victor W. Geraci, "Fess Parker Winery: Family Hospitality" (Seminar Biosketch, University of California Santa Barbara, 1995), passim.

[14] Interview with Barbara Banke by Richard P. Ryba, 11 February 1994; Dan Berger, "Tepusquet Vineyard sold in joint deal," *Santa Barbara News-Press*, 3 July 1987; Kathleen Sharp, "Northern operations expand southward," *The New York Times*, 17 June 1990; Tim Tesconi, "Vintage Success," *Santa Barbara News-Press*, 26 June 1995.

[15] Betty Williams's *The Third Leaf* recorded the groundbreaking in photos and prose; Beverly J. Schwartzberg, "Buttonwood Farm Winery: Working With Nature" (Seminar Biosketch, University of California Santa Barbara, 1995), passim.

[16] "Planners consider rules for county's wineries," *Goleta Valley Today*, 30 September 1974; Santa Barbara County Environmental Quality Commission, *Environmental Quality Report 74-EIR-15, for the Santa Ynez Winery, Santa Ynez, California* (Santa Barbara, California: 1974), 1.

[17] "Winery operations allowed in farmland preserve areas," *Santa Barbara News-Press*, 27 June 1977.

[18] " Planners oppose proposal on mobile home tract sale," *Santa Barbara News-Press*, 28 May 1982.

[19] Interview with Richard Sanford by Victor W. Geraci and Otis L. Graham, Jr., 3 March 1995; Sarah Harper Case, "Sanford Winery: Commitment to Quality" (Seminar Biosketch, University of California Santa Barbara, 1995), passim.

[20] Interview with Jim Clendenen by Richard P. Ryba, 10 February 1994; Sarah Harper Case, "Au Bon Climat: Not Anti-tech . . . Just Realistic," (Seminar Biosketch, University of California Santa Barbara, 1995), passim.

[21] Jay Stuller, "Hollywood and Vine: Making the Most of an Image," *Hemisphere* (January 1995), 92.

[22] Beverly J. Schwartzberg, "Whitcraft Winery: Radio's Wine Host Turns to Quality" (Seminar Biosketch, University of California Santa Barbara, 1995), passim; Sarah Harper Case, "John Kerr Winery: An Independent Spirit" (Seminar Biosketch, University of California Santa Barbara, 1995), passim; Susan Goldstein, "Mosby Winery: A Family Affair" (Seminar Biosketch, University of California Santa Barbara, 1995), passim; Susan Goldstein, "Lane Tanner: Keeper of the Grapes" (Seminar Biosketch, University of California Santa Barbara, 1995), passim.

[23] Interview with Kate Firestone by Victor W. Geraci, 3 February 1994.

[24] Interview with Hayley Firestone Jessup by Victor W. Geraci, 3 February 1994; Interview with Kate Firestone by Victor W. Geraci, 3 February 1994; Geraci, "Fess Parker Winery: Family Hospitality" (Seminar Biosketch, University of California Santa Barbara, 1995), passim.

[25] "Dim outlook for wine growers," *Los Angeles Times*, 21 October 1980; *Los Angeles Times*, 26 May 1983; Tim Tesconi, "Family winery grows into empire," *Santa Barbara News-Press*, 26 June 1995, 1, 2.

[26] "Big wineries head south," *Santa Barbara News-Press*, 19 June 1988.

[27] Interview with Boyd Bettencourt by Beverly J. Schwartzberg, 29 July 1995.

[28] California Agricultural Statistical Service, *California Wine Grape Acreage 1980-90* (Sacramento: California Department of Agriculture).

[29] Gomberg, Fredrikson & Associates, *The*

Wine Industry's Contribution, 1994, 3.

30 "Viticultural Area of the South Central Coast," *Wine Spectator,* 15 December 1989.

31 Lon Fletcher quote in the *Santa Barbara News-Press,* 17 September 1994.

32 Interview with Jess Jackson by Richard Ryba, 11 February 1994.

33 "Prudential Insurance sells Sierra Madre vineyard," *Los Padres Sun,* 17 August 1988; "Vineyard sold for $8.5 million," *Santa Barbara News-Press,* 19 August 1988; Interview with Dale Hampton by Victor W. Geraci and Susan Goldstein, 10 February 1994.

34 Rich Cartiere, Teri Shore, and Marshall Farrer. "Calif.'s 'Vineyard Royalty Doubles Holdings," *Wine Business Monthly* (May 1996), 1, 11.

35 "Area growers see green: vintage prices are toasted," *Santa Barbara News-Press,* 14 October 1988.

36 Jeff Newton, telephone interview by Victor W. Geraci, November 1994.

37 Interview with Richard Sanford by Victor W. Geraci and Otis L. Graham Jr., 7 March 1995; Interview with Jim Clendenen by Richard P. Ryba, 10 February 1994; Interview with Stephan Bedford by Victor W. Geraci, 24 February 1994; Interview with Bob Miller by

Richard P. Ryba, 15 September 1994.

38 "A winery in the making," *New York Times,* 23 July 1978; "Vintner bubbles about capitol business," *Santa Barbara News-Press,* 12 February 1981; Interview with Fred Brander by Beverly J. Schwartzberg, 8 April 1994.

39 Wendell C. Lee, *United States Viticultural Areas* (San Francisco: The Wine Institute, 1992); Interview with Bob Miller by Richard P. Ryba, 15 September 1994.

40 Matt Kramer, *Making Sense of California Wine,* 9, 11-14.

Chapter 5

1 Gomberg, Fredrikson & Associates, *The Wine Industry's Economic Contribution to Santa Barbara County* (San Francisco: Gomberg, Fredrikson & Associates, 1997), 5, 7.

2 Ibid., 4, 5.

3 Martha Groves, "The road to grapeness: California wineries pour their efforts into building reputation overseas," *Los Angeles Times,* 26 June 1996, D-1, D-6.

4 Bob Senn, "Grapevine," *Santa Barbara Independent,* 27 October 1994; Jay Stuller, "Hollywood and Vine," *Hemispheres* (January 1995), 92; Interview with Jim Clendenen by Richard P. Ryba, 10 February 1994.

5 Gomberg, Fredrikson & Associates, *The Wine Industry's Contribution,* 1994, 7.

6 Frank J. Prial, "Wine Talk," *New York Times,* 28 February 1996, B7.

7 Bob Senn, "Getting into the spirit," *Santa Barbara Independent,* 7 December 1995, 29.

8 *Wines and Vines* (February 1988), 20; Susan Goldstein, "Andrew Murray Vineyards" (Seminar Biosketch, University of California Santa Barbara, 1995), passim; Nora K. Wallace, "Winemaker has a taste for adventure," *Santa Barbara News-Press,* 1 October 1994; David Baum, "These Golden Vineyards: How Did Santa Barbara Wines Get So Good So Fast?" *Santa Barbara Magazine* (July/August 1992), 30-35.

9 "Alumni of winery are brought back to produce special series," *Santa Barbara News-Press,* 27 August 1994; Baum, "These Golden Vineyards," 33.

10 "Grapevine," *Wine Spectator* (30 April 1996, vol. 21, no.1), 11; *The Wine Advocate* (Issue 87, 26 June 1993); Santa Barbara County Vintners Association release, 17 July 1992; *The Wine Spectator* (15 July 1993), 20-21; Dennis Schaefer, "County wines top Eclipse list," *Santa Barbara News-Press,* 17 February 1995; Steve Pitcher, "Sanford Winery's Chardonnay tops the taste-off," *San Francisco Chronicle,* 19 January 1994, 4;

Robert Parker, *Food and Wine* (September 1993), passim.

[11] Otis L. Graham, interview with sales-clerk in The Wine Specialist, 4 February 1994, Washington, D.C.

Chapter 6

[1] "U.S. wine exports continue heady growth of a decade," *Los Angeles Times* (4 May 1997), B2; Quentin Hardy, "Wine and women," *The Wall Street Journal* (7 April 1997), 1.

[2] John Elson, "The Wine Portfolio," *Time* (4 July 1994), passim; Gavin Power and Glen Martin, "Big trouble in vineland," *San Francisco Chronicle*, 3 August 1994, 1, 9-10.

[3] *San Francisco Chronicle*, 3 August 1994; Interview with Stephan Bedford by Victor W. Geraci, 24 February 1994; Mark Van De Kamp, "Ballard vineyard beset by phylloxera," *Santa Barbara News-Press*, 15 July 1995; Clive Irving, "Juice Valley," *Conde Nast Traveler* (November 1992).

[4] Mark Van De Kamp, "Ballard vineyard beset by phylloxera," *Santa Barbara News-Press*, 15 July 1995; "1992 Vineyards Under Seige," *Wine Spectator* (30 April 1996, vol. 21, no. 1), 85.

[5] "Toasting a Long Life: Special Report on Wine and Good Health," *Wine Spectator* (15 March 1994), 47-48; "Red Wines Propelled California Wine Shipments,"

Wines and Vines, (July 1993), 26; David N. Whitten and Martin Lipp, *To Your Health! Two Physicians Explore the Health Benefits of Wine* (New York: Harper Collins West, 1994), passim; Laura Shapiro, "To Your Health," *Newsweek* (22 January 1996, Vol. 127), 52-54; "1979 Breakthroughs in Wine and Health," *Wine Spectator* (30 April 1996, vol. 21, no. 1), 59; "1995 More Wine, More Health," *Wine Spectator* (30 April 1996, vol. 21, no. 1).

[6] Tin Unwin, *Wine and the Vine: A Historical Geography of Viticulture and the Wine Trade* (New York: Routledge, 1991), 45.

[7] Clive Irving "Juice Valley," *Conde Nast Traveler* (November 1992), 118; Vicki Leon, *California Wineries: San Luis Obispo, Santa Barbara and Ventura* (San Luis Obispo, Calif.: Blake Publications, 1986), 2.

[8] "The green legacy," *The New York Times*, 9 January 1965, 24.

[9] Jim Brewer and Elliot Diringer, "Sonoma County's growing pains," *San Francisco Chronicle*, 24 March 1986, 1, 4.

[10] Irving, "Juice Valley," 118; Jeff Morgan, "California's Wide Open Spaces," *Wine Spectator* (15 May 1996), 49; Leon, *California Wineries*, 6.

BIBLIOGRAPHY

PUBLISHED SOURCES

Books

Adams, Leon D. *The Wines of America.* New York: McGraw-Hill, 1985.

Amerine, Maynard Andrew, and V. L. Singleton. *Wine: An Introduction for Americans.* Los Angeles: University of California Press, 1972.

Balzer, Robert Lawrence. *The Los Angeles Times Book of California Wines.* New York: Harry N. Abrams, Inc., 1984.

Bancroft, Hubert Howe. *The Works of Hubert Howe Bancroft, Volume XXXIV, California Pastoral 1769-1848.* San Francisco: The History Company, 1888.

Bank of America. *California Wine Outlook: An Economic Study of the California Wine and Wine Grape Industries,* September 1973.

Blumberg, Robert S., and Hurst Hannum. *The Fine Wines of California.* New York: Doubleday & Company, 1971.

Board of State Viticultural Commissioners. *Directory of the Grape Growers, Wine Makers and Distillers.* Sacramento: State of California, 1891.

Bynum, Lindley. *California Wines: How To*

Enjoy Them. Los Angeles: Homer H. Boelter Lithography, 1955.

Caire, Helen. *Santa Cruz Island: A History and Recollections of an Old California Rancho.* Spokane: The Arthur H. Clark Company, 1993.

Coombs, Gary B., ed. *Those Were the Days: Landmarks of Old Goleta.* Goleta, Calif.: Institute for American Research, 1986.

Conaway, James. *Napa.* New York: Houghton Mifflin, 1990.

Carosso, Vincent P. *The California Wine Industry, 1830-1895: A Study of the Formative Years.* Los Angeles: University of California Press, 1951.

Fay, James S., senior ed. *California Almanac: 5th Edition.* Santa Barbara, Calif.: Pacific Data Resources (ABC-Clio), 1991.

Gomberg, Fredrikson & Associates. *The Wine Industry's Economic Contribution to Santa Barbara County.* San Francisco: Gomberg, Fredrikson & Associates, 1994 and 1997.

Haley, Brian D. *Aspects and Social Impacts and Organization in the Recently Developed Wine Industry of Santa Barbara County, California.* Santa Barbara, Calif.: Center For Chicano Studies, 1989.

Johnson, Hugh. *Vintage: The Story of*

Wine. New York: Simon and Schuster, 1989.

Jones, Idwal. *Vines In the Sun.* New York: William Morrow, 1949.

Kaufman, William I. *Encyclopedia of American Wine.* Los Angeles: Houghton Mifflin Company, 1985.

Kramer, Matt. *Making Sense of California Wines.* New York: William Morrow, 1992.

Mason, Jesse D. *History of Santa Barbara County, California.* Oakland: Thompson and West, 1993.

Melville, John. *Guide to California Wines.* San Carlos, Calif.: Nourse Publishing Company, 1960.

Millner, Cork. *Vintage Valley: The Wineries of Santa Barbara County.* Santa Barbara, Calif.: McNally & Loftin, 1983.

Muscatine, Doris, Maynard A. Amerine, and Bob Thompson. *The University of California/Sotheby Book of California Wine.* Los Angeles: University of California Press, 1984.

Peninou, Ernest P., and Sidney S. Greenleaf. *A Directory of California Wine Growers and Wine Makers in 1860.* Berkeley: Tamalpais Press, 1967.

Pinney, Thomas. *A History of Wine In America: From the Beginnings to*

Prohibition. Los Angeles: University of California Press, 1989.

Rorabaugh, W. J. *The Alcoholic Republic: An American Tradition.* New York: Oxford University Press, 1979.

Simpson, Sir George. *An Overland Journey Round the World, During the Years 1841 and 1842.* Philadelphia: Lee and Blanchard, 1847.

Sullivan, Charles L. *Like Modern Edens: Winegrowing in Santa Clara Valley and Santa Cruz Mountains 1798-1981.* Cupertino, Calif.: California History Center, De Anza College, 1982.

Teiser, Ruth, and Catherine Harroun. *Wine Making in California.* New York: McGraw-Hill, 1983.

Thompson, Bob, ed. *California Wine Country.* Menlo Park, Calif.: Lane Books, 1969.

Tompkins, Walker A. *Goleta: The Good Land.* San Francisco: Pioneer, 1976.

_____. *It Happened in Old Santa Barbara.* Santa Barbara, Calif.: Santa Barbara National Bank, 1976.

_____. *Santa Barbara History Makers.* Santa Barbara, Calif.: McNally and Loftin, 1983.

Tyrrell, Ian R. *Sobering Up: From Temperance to Prohibition in Antebellum America, 1800–1860.* Westport, Conn.:

Greenwood Press, 1979.

Unwin, Tim. *Wine and the Vine: An Historical Geography of Viticulture and the Wine Trade.* New York: Routledge, 1991.

Articles

Amerine, Maynard A. "An Introduction to the Pre-Repeal History of Grapes and Wines in California," *Agricultural History* 63 (April 1969): 259-268.

Baum, David. "These Golden Vineyards: How Did Santa Barbara Get So Good So Fast?" *Santa Barbara Magazine* (July/August 1992), 30–35.

Bowman, J. N. "The Vineyards of Provincial California," *Wine Review* (April, May, and June 1943), passim.

Burden, Annette. "Pride of the Valley." *Santa Barbara Magazine* (November/December 1983), 39–53.

Millner, Cork. "Tours and Tasting." *Santa Barbara Magazine* (November/December 1983), 39–46, 64–65.

Paris, Ellen. "Santa Ynez Valley, California Grape Expectations." *Relax Magazine* (August 1993), 49–53, 70–73.

Caire, Helen. "Santa Cruz Island Vintage." *Noticias.* (Spring\Summer 1989), 143–151.

"Santa Ynez Valley Issue." *Noticias*

(Autumn 1962), 1–19.

Newspapers

Los Angeles Times

New York Times

Santa Barbara Independent

Santa Barbara News-Press

UNPUBLISHED WORKS

Days, Mary Louise, "Mission Vineyards and San Jose Vineyard: A Relic of Mission Times." June 13, 1986.

ORAL INTERVIEWS

Craig Addis
Ralph Aufderheide
Tony Austin
Bryan Babcock
Barbara Banke
Stephan Bedford
Norman Beko
Boyd and Claire Hunt-Bettencourt
Sharon Blewis
David Block
Frederic Brander
Dean Brown
Ken Brown
Michael Brown
Jim Clendenen
Bret Davenport
Richard Doré
Sherrill Duggan
A. Brooks Firestone
Kate Firestone
Hayley Firestone Jessup
Brian Haley
Dale Hampton
T. Hayer
Ed Holt
David & Margy Houtz
Jess Jackson
Barry Johnson
John Kerr
Mel Knox
Pierre Lafond
Bob Lindquist
Rick Longoria
Louis Lucas
Bruce McGuire
Kim McPherson

Jeff Maiken
Donna Marks
Bob Miller
Bill and Geraldine Mosby
Jim and Fran Murray
Jeff Newton
Katie O'Hara
Charles Ortman
Pam Maines Ostendorf
Eli Parker
Fess Parker
Harold Pfeiffer
Laila Rashid
Fred Rice
Richard Sanford
Douglas Scott
Lane Tanner
Bill Wathen
Chris Whitcraft
Art White
Jeff Wilkes
Betty Williams
Bob and Jeanne Woods
David Yager

PHOTOGRAPHY CREDITS

Kirk Irwin: front and back covers; cover flaps; half-title (i); title (ii, iii); contents (all, v); vi; vii; viii; ix; x; xi; xii-1; 2, upper left; 3; 4; 6; 7; 9; 12-13; 17; 18-19; 21; 22, both; 24, upper left; 26, both; 27; 30; 31, both; 32-33; 34; 35; 36; 37, upper right; 38, all; 39; 40, both; 42, left; 43, both; 44; 45, both; 46; 47, both; 48-49; 50, all; 51, both; 52, bottom; 54, both; 55, both; 56-57; 58, both; 59, both; 60, all; 61; 77, all.

In order of appearance, by page number:
2, lower inset: Santa Barbara Historical Society; **5, both:** Santa Barbara Historical Society; **8, lower left:** Santa Barbara Winery; **8, upper right:** Goleta Chamber of Commerce; **10, middle column:** Ventura County Museum of History and Art; **10, right column, top and middle:** Santa Cruz Island Foundation; **10, right column, bottom:** Santa Barbara Historical Society; **14:** Lompoc Valley Chamber of Commerce, with permission of Dan Sawatsky and Lompoc Mural Society; **15, both:** with permission of the Alfonso family, © 1997 Jim Norris; **20, upper left:** Chris Neely private collection; **20, lower right:** Santa Barbara Winery; **23, both:** *Santa Maria Times*, Karen White; **24, lower right:** Mosby Winery; **25:** Firestone Vineyard; **28, wine label:** *Santa Maria Times*, Karen White; **28, lower right:** Santa Barbara County Vintners' Association (SBCVA); **29, left:** Rick Longoria; **29, right:** *Santa Maria Times*, Karen White; **37, lower left:** SBCVA; **41:** SBCVA; **42, right:** SBCVA; **52, top:** Zaca Mesa Winery; **53:** SBCVA

ACKNOWLEDGMENTS

This history is the work of the eighteenth class in the Graduate Program in Public Historical Studies, University of California, Santa Barbara. Although each of us participated fully in the research, thinking, and writing that went into this book, which is a collaborative product, individual members of the team had primary responsibility for certain portions. Beverly J. Schwartzberg led the analysis of the early Santa Barbara and California wine industry, while Victor W. Geraci focused on the California story from Prohibition through the 1960s. Sarah Harper Case and Richard P. Ryba were principally responsible for the decades of the 1970s and 1980s, and Susan Goldstein concentrated on the 1990s. Professor Otis L. Graham, Jr. served as the principal investigator, with administrative and production assistance from Victor W. Geraci.

Special thanks goes to Lindsey Reed, whose expertise and professionalism has guided most public history classes in the production process. Public History secretary Janet Stone was always there to provide coordination and support for the long-term project.

A number of people contributed a significant amount of their time to help us complete this project. Sue DeLapa of the *Santa Barbara News-Press,* Mary Louise Days of the City of Santa Barbara Planning Department, Michael Redmon of the Santa Barbara Historical Society, and Lori Ritchie of Special Collections at the UCSB Library all offered invaluable assistance in our research efforts. Ideas and materials for research were provided by the friendly staff of the Wine Institute and Arel Borg, chief librarian of Amerine Library, University of California, Davis.

The Santa Barbara County Vintners' Association (SBCVA) provided a generous grant that aided the project. Pam Maines Ostendorf, executive director of the SBCVA, supplied the organizational enthusiasm to start and finish the project with the aid of administrative assistant, Jan Skaling. The SBCVA History Committee provided invaluable information and directional guidance throughout the term of the project. Association representatives Richard Sanford, Jeff Maiken, Sherrill Duggan, and Stephan Bedford deserve a special mention for the numerous hours they devoted to the completion of the book. Several industry people graciously allowed us to interview them, and their names can be found in the bibliography. They all greatly aided our work, but are in no way responsible for our views.

David Yager's insights on the role of the county in planning for wineries greatly aided that section of the manuscript. Finally, we wish to express our appreciation to Thomas Pinney and Elizabeth Koed for reading an earlier draft of this book and giving us their helpful comments.